Gender and Society in Contemporary Brazilian Cinema

DAVID WILLIAM FOSTER

Gender and Society in Contemporary Brazilian Cinema

University of Texas Press, Austin

First edition, 1999

Requests for permission to reproduce material from this work should
be sent to Permissions, University of Texas Press, Box 7819, Austin,
TX 78713-7819.

∞The paper used in this book meets the minimum requirements of
ANSI/NISO Z39.48-1992 (R1997) (Permanence of Paper).

Library of Congress Cataloging-in-Publication Data

Foster, David William.
    Gender and society in contemporary Brazilian cinema / David
William Foster — 1st ed.
        p.   cm.
    Includes bibliographical references and index.
    ISBN 0-292-72509-4 (hardcover : alk. paper)
    ISBN 0-292-72510-8 (pbk. : alk. paper)
    1. Motion pictures—Brazil—History.   2. Sex role in motion
pictures.   I. Title.
    PN1993.5.B6   F67   1999
    791.43'653—dc21
                                                            99-6147

This book is dedicated to the Brazilians whose friendship has, during the past two decades, convinced me that I want Brazil to be an integral part of my personal and professional life: Roberto Reis,† Denize Araujo, Hamilton Lobo, Joe Bonilauri, Robson Corrêa de Camargo, Adriana Ferreira, André Carreira, Silvana Garcia, Carlos Caldart, and Jaime Guinzburg. And to those students, colleagues, and associates who help me keep all this scholarly work lots and lots of fun.

Contents

Acknowledgments

I wish to acknowledge the support of various programs for research at Arizona State University that have, for thirty years now, generously supported my work on Latin American culture. My research assistants for this project have included Gastón Alzate, Oscar Díaz, Kanishka Sen, Camille Villafañe, Alvaro Vergara-Mery, and Sandy Quinn. Clarice Deal served as a generous consultant on questions relating to the Portuguese language and Brazilian culture. Robson Corrêa de Camargo provided me with valuable sociohistorical and political information. Denize Correa Araujo and Melissa Fitch Lockhart offered valuable critical readings of the manuscript. Eva Bueno made invaluable suggestions regarding social and historical facts of Brazilian culture. Daniel Altamiranda, as always, assisted me with sharply analytical readings of my expositions. Robson Corrêa de Camargo, Denize Araujo, Hamilton Lobo, and Joe Bonilauri helped me obtain many of the films necessary for this study.

Gender and Society in Contemporary Brazilian Cinema

.

Introduction

Brazilian cinema, along with Mexican, Argentine, and to a great extent Cuban filmmaking, is one of the most extensive in Latin America. As in the case of Argentina and Mexico, Brazilian cinema got its start in the mid-1890s as part of the enormous interest in the manifestations of modernity on the part of important Latin American societies and the equally enormous interest on the part of European commercial ventures to take advantage of emerging Latin American marketplaces. By the second decade of the twentieth century, Brazil had an extensive array of movie houses and a local production to service the demand they created. Just like other Latin American countries (and, indeed, most countries in the world), Brazil also experienced the vagaries of the nascent industry, especially the difficult relationship between national and foreign production. Early national production, which had become quite healthy by the end of the second decade, was seriously affected by the shift in the distribution sector from buying foreign films for local exhibition to renting them.

As an extension of the interest in foreign products created by the project of modernity, when foreign movies became readily available and inexpensive as rentals, national production was seriously damaged; since that time the history of filmmaking in Brazil, as in other countries, has shown many attempts to come to terms with how to balance a national production with foreign imports. Because of the considerable expense involved in filmmaking, as opposed to other forms of cultural production, it has been necessary historically to combine government subsidies for film production, usually through a national film institute or a program for formal underwriting—Embrafilme in Brazil, for example—with formal restrictions on foreign imports and projection quotas. Extreme cases, such as the disappearance of government subsidies in Argentina in the current decade or the strict regulation of foreign imports in Fidel Castro's Cuba, have rarely occurred in Brazil (an excellent, though now outdated, historical survey of filmmaking in Brazil is provided by Dennis West, *Contemporary Brazilian Cinema;* more recent filmmaking is covered by Robert Stam and Ismail Xavier, "Transformation of National Allegory").

In the case of Brazil, the two greatest periods of internal support have been the period of the Cinema Novo in the early 1960s and the period of redemocratization that began in 1985. According to John King, "between 1956 and 1961 industrial production increased by 80 per cent" (*Magical Reels,* 105); thanks to the extent to which filmmaking tapped into the prevailing nationalism of the period and concepts of the inherent greatness of Brazil and its manifest destiny in the international arena, the Cinema Novo became probably the only truly international movement in Latin American filmmaking. Usually associated with the name of one director, Glauber Rocha (1938–1981), the Cinema Novo, which recycled with a Brazilian accent major aspects of postwar Neorealism, focused on rural themes in some of its most famous texts (e.g., Rui [also often seen as Ruy] Guerra's *Os fuzis* [The Guns, 1964], Glauber Rocha's *Barravento* [1962], Nelson Pereira dos Santos's *Vidas secas* [Dry Lives, 1963], and Lima Barreto's *O cangaceiro* [The Bandit, 1953], perhaps the most famous Brazilian film of all time). Such a focus tended to serve as a platform for the representation of social and political themes in Brazilian society, especially the ways in which abiding conditions of non-urban life, particularly in the deeply impoverished Northeast, constituted a continuing gap between daily material conditions of life and the ideologemes of Brazil's national greatness. Such a focus, in turn, established links with committed filmmaking in other parts of Latin America that were concerned with the struggle against the neocolonialism that, although still tied to European sources in many respects, was increasingly identified with United States interests.

This was particularly true in the case of Brazil, where the economic dominance that resulted from ties to the United States during World War II resulted in a Brazilian economy that was particularly overshadowed by U.S. influence in the late 1950s, the period out of which the Cinema Novo emerged (see the discussion below on the image of U.S.-centered capitalism in *Ópera do malandro* [Rogue's Opera, 1986], which was made by Rui Guerra, one of the great Cinema Novo directors). The measures of repressive censorship imposed in the early 1970s by the military government that came to power by coup in 1964 essentially put an end to the Cinema Novo.

The Cinema Novo also produced important urban-oriented titles which showed the impact of influences such as Italian post–World War II Neorealism (e.g., Rui Guerra's *Os cafajestes* [The Hustlers, 1963]). The effective combination of a documentary or quasi-documentary content, elements of folklore and autochthonous mythology, and a highly auteurial style of the filmic structure of photography combined to bring to the Cinema Novo a level of professionalism and artistic creativity that ensured worldwide attention (one of the best sources on the Cinema Novo is Randal Johnson's *Cinema Novo × 5*).

The Cinema Novo, matching similar interests in fiction and to a lesser extent theater, was the last great manifestation of a non-urban cultural production in Latin America. During the first half of the twentieth century, as Latin America became more and more a continent of metropolitan life (foreshadowing the subsequent emergence of megalopolises like Mexico City and São Paulo), cultural production, while not ignoring the city, continued to focus predominantly on non-urban culture. It promoted the prevailing belief that cities were somehow an accident (after all, most of them were reflexes of the Spanish and Portuguese empires which national independence and cultural nationalism had repudiated in the nineteenth century) and that a "true" national identity was to be found in the countryside, whether strictly Creole in nature or alloyed with indigenous, African, and non-Hispanic immigrant elements. This is evident in the great early-twentieth-century Latin American novels: the Mexican Mariano Azuela's *Los de abajo* (1916), the Argentine Ricardo Güiraldes's *Don Segundo Sombra* (1926), the Venezuelan Rómulo Gallegos's *Doña Bárbara* (1929), and the Brazilian João Guimarães Rosa's *Grande sertão: veredas* (Big Plains: Paths; trans. as *The Devil to Pay in the Backlands, 1956*).

The city, however, began to be important in Brazilian culture with the famous Semana de Arte Moderna, which took place in São Paulo in 1922 (see the discussion below of *Eternamente Pagu* [Eternally Pagu, 1987], which has as one of its backdrops cultural and political movements in São Paulo during the 1920s and 1930s); Nelson Pereira dos Santos's documentary *Rio 40 graus* (Rio 40° Latitude, 1955) focused on the city, particularly on the slums, but more typically one associated with the Cinema Novo products like Dos Santos's *Vidas secas*, based on Graciliano Ramos's novel of the same name and referring to the barren Northeast, Rui Guerra's *Os fuzis*, dealing with a peasant uprising and its violent repression by army troops, or Rocha's *Barravento,* the first feature-length Cinema Novo, on fishermen. As King observes: "The city, the bourgeois and the urban proletariat are largely absent from these early films: the privileged space is that of the desolate Northeast of Brazil, the deserted backlands, the *sertão,* with its social bandits, *cangaceiros,* and messianic leaders" (*Magical Reels,* 108).

By contrast, when filmmaking in the early 1980s and particularly after the return to institutional democracy in 1985 gathered momentum in a Brazil that was very much changed from the 1960s, before the military dictatorship, and from the circumstances of cultural production during the dictatorship (1964–1985), urban culture had become the order of the day. Indeed, one recurring theme would be the fate of rural provincials as they swelled the population of major areas in Brazil's demographic economic process, parallel to that of other Latin American cities. São Paulo has doubled in population since the early 1960s, the heyday of the Cinema Novo, and, thirty years later, ranks as the world's third largest city, with approximately 19 million inhabitants. The material conditions of life may have changed little in the *sertão* since Rocha, Guerra, and Dos Santos made their films, but the individuals they describe have, in massive waves of internal migration, made their way to the city. It is the circumstances of their life there that Brazilian filmmakers are now constrained to describe: Suzana Amaral in *A hora da estrela* (The Hour of the Star, 1985), for example. Concomitantly, other films deal with social groups in the city (Rui Guerra's *Ópera do malandro*), definitions of individual identity against the backdrop of the city (Paolo Thiago's *Jorge um brasileiro* [Jorge, a Brazilian, 1989]), unique social problems of the city (Bruno Barreto's *O beijo no asfalto* [Kiss on the Asphalt, 1981—a film from the period of transition]), women's history (Norma Bengell's *Eternamente Pagu*), and urban guerrillas during the dictatorship (Sérgio Rezende's *Lamarca* [1994]).

This monograph is about this second important period of Brazilian filmmaking, a period whose extensive filmography would not be possible were it not for some measure of official support in the face of the enormous challenge offered to national culture by the foreign films that have engaged with the project of neoliberalism that is predicated on massive foreign investments and the massive importation of foreign products in all categories, including culture. Yet there is also the simple fact that, with the disappearance of censorship upon the return to democracy, whole new cultural categories have emerged to compete with local production, not only social-theme films and some action films that could not be viewed in Brazil during the height of censorship for reasons of content, but a whole array of pornography to meet an avid and deprived market (concerning the relationship between filmmaking and the state, see Randal Johnson, *The Film Industry*).

Many Brazilian films have been made in the last decade, as they have been in Argentina and especially in Mexico, which produces vast quantities of films to meet a local popular culture market that can be described as influenced in one way or another by the production codes of Hollywood. Nevertheless, the return to democracy, the suspension of censorship, the development of a bibliography in new areas of social research, the implantation of neoliberal economics, and the crises of the megalopolis have all joined already long-standing issues in Brazilian culture such as racism, uneven development and distribution, classism, corruption, and social injustice to stimulate a strong internal demand for a national cinematographic production that would address these issues.

To be sure, many of these films have vied for international attention, such as Thiago's *Jorge um brasileiro* or more recently Fábio Barreto's *O quatrilho* (The Foursome, 1995), which centers on Italian immigrants in southern Brazil in the nineteenth century and was an Oscar finalist for the best foreign film. But Brazilian film, like Brazilian television, theater, and fiction, appeals essentially to an internal market, with some measure of exportation to external Portuguese-speaking venues. It is only the size of Brazil that has made possible such a level of internal consumption, in the face of a language that has few external venues: Brazilian films must, of course, be subtitled if they are to aspire to distribution elsewhere in Latin America and abroad, and there is now even an insistence by some Latin American film directors (e.g., Brazil's Héctor Babenco) on making films directly in English. Yet, precisely because this internal market is so relatively vast, Brazilian filmmaking continues (with uneven levels of official support) to sustain high quantitative and qualitative levels of production, especially with the continued cultural enthusiasm that has been kept alive during the decade since the return to democracy.

The present monograph concentrates on major documents in Brazilian filmmaking since 1985 with only one exception, for thematic reasons, from the period of transition (by the end of the 1970s, the dictatorship had become less authoritarian: while censorship continued to exist, a degree of expression was possible as long as the military was not attacked directly). However, this is not a history of Brazilian filmmaking since 1985. Brazil continues to have an enormous film output, and the inventory of titles deserving of critical analysis far exceeds the modest selection made for this examination of gender issues.

I have chosen films that, in one way or another, deal with gender issues; such a selection is always arbitrary, personal, and to a certain extent aleatory, especially in view of how much there is to choose from. Chapter 1 deals with "Constructions of Masculinity" (*Jorge um brasileiro, Lamarca, Ópera do malandro, O boto* [The Dolphin, 1987], *Capitalismo selvagem* [Savage Capitalism, 1993], *Yndio do Brasil* [Indian of Brazil, 1995]); Chapter 2 with "Constructions of Feminine and Feminist Identities" (*A hora da estrela, Eternamente Pagu, Que bom te ver viva* [How Nice to See You Alive, 1989], *Bananas Is My Business* [1994]); and Chapter 3 with "Same-Sex Positionings and Social Power" (*Barrela* [Lock-Down, 1990], *O beijo no asfalto, Vera* [1987]). There should be little surprise over the decreasing number of films in the three chapters. It is also not surprising that masculine subjects continue to be the core of Brazilian filmmaking, and this is especially true with films that refer to the political resistance of the 1960s and 1970s. Thus, except for highly commercial films touting conventional images of women as sexual objects, films dealing with women are fewer in number. And there should be little surprise that, in a country like Brazil where homophobia continues to be firmly entrenched, especially as regards the visibility of same-sex desire, there should be so few films in which homoeroticism is dealt with in any significant measure.

Gender is an absolute ground zero for most human societies, something that can never not be present. Even when gender is not the thematic center of a cultural text—and it is, however, usually precisely the center, as can be seen from most advertising, music, television programming, and popular magazines and literature— it is always present in the way in which a language like Portuguese obliges gender identity to be evoked unavoidably in each and every speech act. One cannot not announce one's gender affiliation or that of an interlocutor or third-person referent. Merely to fail to do so, either as a solecism or as a deliberate troping of grammatical structures, produces a queering of speech that requires immediate interpretation as a mistake, a joke, an audacious proposal of alternative sexuality, or an encoding of gender ambiguity (such as one might expect to find in songs by Ney Matogrosso, for example). Paralleling speech, bodies must always be signed as masculine or female, and the complex patterns relating to the division of gender labor in society are necessarily concomitant with such body signatures. The *malandro* in Rui Guerra's *Ópera do malandro* is not a generic designation, but a gendered one, and it would be impossible to conceive of this text allowing for an exchange of roles between men and women, even when the work does, in fact, have a subtext dealing with the issue of phallic women. And Suzana Amaral's *A hora da estrela* is not just about rural provincials struggling for survival in São Paulo, but rather about a woman's story of survival. Of course, there is a masculine figure that is part of this struggle, but it would be inconceivable to confuse Macabea's story with that of Olímpico or to conflate them into one genderless character.

Nevertheless, virtually all of these films thematize gender in one way or another because of the ground-zero importance of gender as an absolute horizon of social subjectivity in Brazil as in all of the West. Even when texts do not frame gender issues as such, gender is all too often used in an allegorical fashion. By this, I mean that personal issues of gender identity, gender conflict and crisis, threats to gender integrity, and gender transgression may all be a way of representing collective concerns that may or may not conventionally and customarily be identified via figures of gender. For example, it is quite common to embody the spiritual values of a nation in feminine figures: England's Britannia, Mexico's Virgin of Guadalupe, or Brazil's Nossa Senhora da Aprecida, the national Virgin Mary figure and patroness of the country. Nossa Senhora da Aprecida is also identified with the rural past; as a "black" religious figure whose mythic or folkloric origins as a miracle worker lie in having been caught in the net of black fishermen in the Paraíba River in the state of São Paulo, she evokes or provokes national racial anxieties. It is perhaps for this reason that, with a significant change of rhetorical register, Brazil's *garota de Ipanema,* white or very lightly mulatto, can be viewed as such a persuasive national feminine type. Indeed, national identity is strongly tied to ideal feminine stereotypes. Yet the destiny of a nation is also frequently conceived in terms of masculine virility and imaged as an appropriate male personification: the U.S.A.'s Uncle Sam, England's John Bull, the mythified Che Guevara for Castro's Cuba, or Mexico's Aztec warrior.

In Brazil, the figure of the "colossus" or the "giant" man (the latter enshrined in a verse of the national anthem) resonates with sexual authority,[1] as in the case of the film analyzed below, *Jorge um brasileiro.* I argue that the hypermasculinity of Paulo Thiago's fictional protagonist in *Jorge um brasileiro* or of the historical protagonist, at least as played by the lead character, in Sérgio Re-zende's *Lamarca* is far from circumstantial. Rather, it is crucial to the construction of meaning in the two films, whereby the gender features of the characters point not just to their roles as social subjects, but to the systems of values and social meaning that their bodies quite literally embody: they are special cases of the social subject in that their stories, as exemplified by the bodies that they display through the visual medium of the film, encode narratives of collective history.

Jorge's behavior—and it seems clear that he is unaware of the meanings Thiago wishes the spectator to associate with it—re-volves around the possibility of an assertive Everyman who will rid himself of subservience and exploitation in the newly redemo-cratized Brazil, and all this in the context of undertaking a semi-epic voyage of self-discovery. By the same token, the emergence of possibilities for women's social and political intervention in the postmilitary period, an emergence that is as important in terms of historical evolution as it is in terms of its symbolic confrontation with the exclusive masculinism of the armed forces that ruled Brazil between 1964 and 1984, legitimizes and provides meaningful contexts for attempts to construct a history of women in Brazil. Norma Bengell's film on Patrícia Galvão (Pagu) is not just the story of one important female revolutionary figure. Rather, the fact that she was Brazil's first female political prisoner during the period of Getúlio Vargas's fascist Estado Novo, the predecessor of the neofascist regime that came to power in 1964, makes Pagu a particularly important female protagonist of Brazilian history to remember in 1987, only two years after the restoration of democracy.

The theoretical premises underlying such an interpretation of the use of gender rely on the belief that gender identity, sexual roles, and even erotic desire are as much complex social constructions as they are constitutive elements of biological bodies. Gender is not exclusively a social construction, nor is it a matter of bio-logical essentialism. One can debate the proportional interaction of the biological and the constructive, but the point is that the body and its subjectivity interact with social circumstances that, therefore, impinge on the body-subjectivity compound so that meaning moves back and forth between them. For this reason, if the individual's identity is determined in a certain measure by interaction with the social text, an interpretive modeling of the individual such as takes place in cultural products has the power to constitute an interpretation of that social text. Indeed, this is so much the case that it does not take an enormous investment in social theories of cultures to understand that a considerable bulk of cultural production is primarily of interest not because of an individual's "unique" story, but rather because of what that story has to say in terms of the social text that we all inhabit. Moreover, like gender, the social text is something that we cannot not inhabit, for even an individual's attempts at separation from the social text say something about the social text that one wishes to renounce, while underscoring the essential impossibility of doing so.

This study is organized under three headings: masculine issues, feminist issues, and issues of gender disruption and transgression. Such an organization is necessarily dictated by the hypostatized nature of gender roles in a society like Brazil, which is certainly not substantially different from the West in general. As a consequence, masculine and feminine concepts tend to be congealed in highly predictable ways in their reference both to individual experience and to the social meaning as well as the allegorical dimensions of that experience. Concomitantly, the semantic load of deviations from overdetermined identities is very heavy, and the slightest variation in the execution of the codes of gender tends to produce violent disruptions in the comings and goings of daily lives, as is evident in the framing of Barreto's *O beijo no asfalto*, where what is claimed to be a gesture of compassion toward a dying man becomes scripted as a dreadful example of homosexuality with terrible, indeed, deadly, repercussions for those involved.

Social semiotic systems are, of course, notoriously unstable, which is why they are so difficult to study and why generalizations are so dangerous. Moreover, the inherent instability of social systems is precisely why such enormous efforts are invested in attempting to hold them firm and steady: if the codes of sexuality, for example, were not so unstable—not so inherently ambiguous and internally contradictory—it would not be necessary for society to concern itself so much with vigilance, enforcement, correction, and chastisement for noncompliance. Thus, part of the issue in the examination of how gender serves as the basis of a sociopolitical allegory must be to investigate both how the process of allegorization reveals, most likely unintentionally, the instability of the very semiotic base it is dealing with and how it creates, again most likely unintentionally, excesses of meaning that can be shown to be problematical for the efficient working of the allegorical proposition at issue. For example, the pairing of men in Guerra's *Ópera do malandro,* while it may be intended to allegorize different historical options for economic exploitation, ends up bringing in a highly charged homosocial relationship between them that at moments veers off toward the homoerotic, as in the staging of the scene that enacts the rivalry between them and later the scene in which one humiliates the other in a game of displaced male rape.

The goal here, then, is not simply to describe selected texts from recent Brazilian filmmaking or only to interpret the ways in which they deal with important issues relevant to the transition from an authoritarian military tyranny to institutional democracy. Rather, an attempt is made to investigate in some detail the semiotic and ideological organization of the films examined and to see how they function as meaningful cultural documents. In the process, it is of importance not to see where they fail (does any cultural document ever really fail in being socially meaningful?—or does any document ever really succeed optimally in the same venture?), but to scrutinize the problems in meaning that derive from the structure, strategies, and procedures—as much specifically filmic as generally cultural—that each director has chosen to pursue. By dealing with these films as ideological texts, I show how each undertakes to "read" sociohistorical reality, in a Marxian sense, in a specifically meaningful way and, moreover, how that reading resonates with—and depends on—gendered human beings whose sexual role is an integral part of the sociohistorical reality.

One last observation: the standard scholarly work on Brazilian filmmaking is *Brazilian Cinema,* edited by Randal Johnson and Robert Stam, published in an expanded edition in 1995 (originally published in 1982). The films I have chosen to discuss are either only mentioned in passing in the final section or not mentioned at all. In this sense, the goal here has been to provide a study that complements and supplements the fine essays in their collection.

CHAPTER I

Constructions
of Masculinity

"Homem tem que ser durão" [*A man's got to be tough*]
—ERASMO CARLOS, SINGER

One of the most intriguing propositions of feminist theory has been not only the rejection of the primacy of the masculine, against which men are judged for their adequacy and women for their noncorrespondence, whether in psychological, sexual, or cultural terms, but the proposition that all gender identity is constructed (see Butler, *Gender Trouble*, for one of the most influential analyses of this proposition). While it has been reasonable for much of the feminist bibliography to concentrate on the construction of the feminine, especially in view of the importance of establishing categorical difference (as opposed to the feminine as viewed as merely the noncorrespondence to the privileged masculine signifier), in recent years, in concert with the rise of queer studies and independently of them, considerable attention has been devoted to how the masculine is constructed and how that identity is maintained, confirmed, overdetermined, and legitimated (see Simpson, *Male Impersonators;* Katz, *The Invention of Heterosexuality*).

Such research is grounded in the axiom that, except for physiological sexual markers, all bodies begin as a clean slate. The many interlocking contexts and situations of social life construct, "inscribe," on the body a complex structure of gender identity. This gender not only involves the sense of individuals belonging to categories of the masculine and feminine, but also involves dimensions of sexual preference. Such a process does not mean that the gender and sexual identity of an individual is only neutrally constructed and is independent of biology. Rather, it means that social processes interact with the body in complex ways such that it is virtually impossible to determine categorically and to isolate what is the consequence of social conditioning and what is the consequence of the intrinsic "wiring" of the body in general and a particular body: e.g., a specific sexual preference may be as much intrinsic to a particular body as it is to factors of social formation. The degree to which this identity conforms to prevailing societal models determines the degree to which a body is in general perceived as normal, and a large part of an individual's social conflicts can derive from the way in which that individual is perceived to be gender/sexual-abnormal and treated accordingly.

From the perspective of gender construction theory, most individuals live their entire lives confirming in multiple and overdetermined ways their adherence to prevailing models, or they spend a good part of their lives dealing with the consequences of being perceived as deviant or unacceptable simulacra of the models endorsed by the hegemonic ideology of gender and sexuality. Since Western, Judeo-Christian society (at least) is obsessed with gender issues, most individuals, if only unconsciously and in compliance with education and programming they have internalized, seek energetically to insure that their gender behavior, their execution of a well-defined gender role, is consistent with the hegemonic ideology and take pains to correct whatever might be viewed as a deviation from it.

It is very evident that, especially in the modern period, there is an abundant amount of cultural production (which has increased geometrically in the past twenty-five years) that addresses cases of sexual deviancy, particularly what is identified as lesbian and gay or what in general falls under the purview of the queer. This includes any disruption in the fulfillment of compulsory monogamous reproductive heterosexuality, which is something like a keyword definition of what for the majority constitutes the prevailing hegemonic ideology of gender and sexuality. From the point of view of the queer as the nonstraight, prostitutes are deviant because they are not monogamous, and even those who are not reproductive (except when nonreproduction is sanctioned by society, as in the case of religious orders) can be called queer, since they do not comply with the mandate to have children. Especially queer are those who are reproductive without being exclusively heterosexual (some homosexuals and some bisexuals). Brazil counts some of the first novels in the West to deal with the queer understood as the nonheterosexual: Adolfo Caminha's male-marked *Bom-crioulo* (trans. as *Bom-Crioulo: The Black Man and the Cabin Boy,* 1895) (see Bueno, "Adolfo Caminha") and the lesbian passage in Aluísio Azevedo's *O cortiço* (The Tenement, 1890).

What is less apparent is the far vaster—indeed, dominant—cultural production where gender construction and maintenance are what the text fundamentally is. Or, if they are not central to the text, they are a significant correlative of the main issue of the text. For example, virtually all films based on the traditional love-story formula transmit, even if never in so many words, a confirmation of established heterosexist roles, with a tightly circumscribed definition of masculine and feminine (see de Lauretis, *Technologies of Gender*). Only in those texts in which there is the suggestion of a deviation from the hegemonic structure might there be an opening toward explicit commentary, as happens in a film like Vincente Minnelli's *Tea and Sympathy* (1956), where a young man's sexual insecurities lead to accusations that he is homosexual; when he is seduced by an older woman, an act of "generosity" that confirms him in his sense of normal masculinity, the specter of sexual irregularity vanishes into thin air. In Brazilian films like Bruno Barreto's *O beijo no asfalto,* discussed in the chapter on same-sex identities, homosexuality is also a specter, but less as the threat of erotic deviancy than as one dimension of power relationships. Thus, the film is never directly about homoeroticism, but rather about the belief that a public kiss awarded a dying man is sexual in nature. The consequences of a spontaneous act that suddenly leaves an individual unprotected in the calculus of power relationships turn out to be the real point of Barreto's film. Since heterosexism and a specific structure of power relations are interdependent—the power that one wields and the power that is wielded against one depend on maintaining a fixed position, whether sexual or some other subsystem correlative, in the social system—the apparent disruption of the form has devastating consequences on the system. By contrast, Fábio Barreto's film *Luzia homem* (Luzia as a Man, 1987) indirectly confirms the gender system and the roles it assigns by demonstrating how an exception may be allowed Luzia for purposes of revenge.[1] However, once that revenge is accomplished, she is obliged to return to her "proper" gender role. Luzia's parents have been slaughtered by marauding bandits; in order to avenge their death, she crossdresses as a man, since it is only as a man that she can garner the symbolic power necessary to settle the blood debt of her parents' killers. Revenge is a masculine undertaking, and Luzia as a woman would have been unable to garner the support of society in her undertaking. Therefore, there can be no question of Luzia's sexual identity, of her sexual persona and its preferences, and the film clearly shows her resumption of conventional femininity in her exchange of male dress for female attire when the debt has been settled: the hegemonic structure naturally and easily reclaims her allegiance. Moreover, Luzia's "true" sexual identity is confirmed by the heterosexual relations she has with a man during the course of the film. Luzia is no Annie Oakley, whose male attire (as Ethel Merman knew very well) was an integral part of a sustained sexual dissidence unknown to the Brazilian farm girl.

There have been extremely few Brazilian films to explore sexual dissidence, whether in terms of gender role, sexual identity, or the conduct and acts of a resistant sexual preference. In the case of Marco Antonio Cury's *Barrela* (see Chapter 3), the violently imposed and sustained homosociality of the jailhouse is crisscrossed with homosexual rape, literal and displaced, as a form of social control in both its horizontal (among prisoners) and vertical (between prisoners and their guards/jailers/police) dimensions. But homosexual rape is not homoeroticism, no matter how hard it may be to separate the two at times (rape may be accompanied by desire and pleasure, and an erotic fantasy may figure rape or something approximating it as desirable). *Barrela* leaves no room for any question of desire, much less love. In the sequence involving male prostitution, the suggestion that the prostitute is a prostitute because of a possibility of satisfying same-sex desire can only end up subscribing to the proposition of male rape as the suppression of desire by violent domination.

Homosocialism is, of course, the norm in Brazilian society and, as a direct extension, in Brazilian cultural production; it is especially evident in privileged realms such as the military, sports, the workplace, and leisure in general. Other men are vital in the maintenance of one's masculine identity. Sexual performance with women and their confirmation of one's virility are clearly crucial, and the production of children is a confirmation of proper masculinity: a pregnant wife or lover is customarily the proudest, albeit transitory, trophy of his masculinity a man can display to the world. Yet, in the day-to-day commerce of society, of much more ongoing value is the ability to relate properly and securely to other men, who, in their acceptance, provide feedback to the man that he is sufficiently masculine. Moreover, although vigilance and enforcement of social conformity, and, in this case, all-important gender conformity, occur in all contexts of an individual's life experience, two are of special importance: the workplace, where the individual spends a large percentage of waking hours; and places of leisure, where a good amount of the rest of the day is spent.

Of these leisure spaces, bars and sports fields and arenas are particularly important. Indeed, in much of Latin America, for most middle and lower sectors of society, allegiance to a soccer team is typically of greater importance than political or religious allegiance, and part of the definition of gender identity through sports involves questioning, in ways that are either heavy-handedly humorous or openly assertive and aggressive, the gender compliance (they are all weak men) or the sexual preference (they are all fags) of the supporters of rival teams. It is in this way that one can understand the strident controversies that surround any hint of same-sex transactions in male sports, such as the general suggestion of displaced homoeroticism made by Juan José Sebreli (*Fútbol y masas*), following the model of American interpretation of football, or the outrage in Argentina in mid-1995 over homosexuals among the ranks of the Selección Nacional team. That the rule of ten percent was applied (the proposition drawn from Alfred Kinsey's work fifty years ago on establishing percentages of homosexual and heterosexual activity and adopted by many gay rights organizations) only increased the outrage. An advertising agency, sympathetic to the gay rights movement, published the image of gays under the legend "Nosotros también nos queremos y nos bañamos juntos" (We also like/love each other and bathe together; note the crucial ambiguity of *queremos* in Spanish), which brought a welcome sense of comic relief to the rumble, although discussion continues to take place as to whether certain signs of affection and patterns of touching, especially in order to congratulate players on successful plays, are appropriate to the gender image athletes ought to maintain and support.

Jorge um brasileiro

> The cinematic male bond might best be described as an unresolvable process that (re)produces freeze frames. . . . Built on the bankability of two male stars, the buddy film negotiates crises of masculine identity centered on questions of class, race, and sexual orientation, by affirming dominant cultural and institutional apparati. (Fuchs, "The Buddy Politic," 195)

Paulo Thiago's 1989 *Jorge um brasileiro,* as opposed to readier treatments drawn from sports or from movies made about the military (e.g., Rui Guerra's legendary 1964 Cinema Novo production *Os fuzis* or Sérgio Rezende's eponymous 1994 film about the revolutionary leader Carlos Lamarca—see analysis below), is exceptional in that it deals with masculinity in the workplace. One must hastily affirm that Thiago's film neither questions the project of masculinity nor demonstrates any significant deviation from it: it has neither feminist nor queer dimensions, except to the degree to which one might wish to claim that any film that showcases hypermasculinity does, in fact, veer toward the edges of the gay and the queer. This is because, in conventional gender ideology, man's body is the neutral and privileged point of reference. Therefore, there is no focus on that body unless it deviates from the norm; put differently, the normal body requires no analysis, since it is simply there as the unquestioned and unexamined anchor of the system of gender meaning. By contrast, the deviant male body and all female bodies are susceptible to scrutiny, precisely to the degree to which they are problematical.

These bodies must be examined, corrected, normalized. The female body is available either categorically to affirm a secure social system through a secure family system or to undermine the family system through its easily occurring lack of proper discipline: *chercher la femme*. Because of the exceptional display of the female body and the enormous gender, sexual, sociopolitical, and economic semiosis that it is required to bear, cultural production overwhelmingly centers on the woman, as feminist criticism, film criticism in particular, has underscored (see Silverman, *The Subject of Semiotics*). Gay and queer bodies bear scrutiny because they, like female bodies as a whole, constitute deviations from the norm. Still, it is obvious that what is at issue are forms of sexual dissidence in which there are immediately evident traces of the deviance. Moreover, it is almost always assumed that any form of sexual deviance will ultimately result in overt manifestation, something like the Dorian Gray Principle of Queerness, with AIDS in recent years fulfilling that function: it was not until Rock Hudson was clearly dying of AIDS that it became impossible to deny the long-standing rumor that he was gay, since his public embodiment was so manifestly in conformance with a normalized masculinity (see Meyer, "Rock Hudson's Body").

Hypermasculinity does present serious semiotic problems. For if it highlights what are considered to be appropriate male features, to be found to a less dramatic degree in regular, everyday men, hypermasculinity calls attention to the male body precisely because of the exaggeration of those features that are most often associated with homoerotic fetishes, such as the sculptured body (highlighted by close-fitting or cut-down clothes), swaggering mannerisms, and a general attitude of cool control and dominance, as one might find in the paradigmatic Tom of Finland drawings. It is for this reason that the hypermasculinity of a Rock Hudson is particularly ironic when viewed from the perspective of an out-of-the-closet gay consciousness and the AIDS epidemic, as is that of the young Marlon Brando, the always young James

Dean, and the oiled-body legions that followed Charlton Heston into battle (see the documentary on gays and lesbians in film: *The Celluloid Closet* [1996], based on Russo's book of the same name). Thus, there is an overdetermination of masculine attributes that results in exactly the sort of excessive display that is the essence of fetishism. How this becomes a problem in Thiago's movie is dealt with below in terms of the disjunction between the title character's body and the average-type bodies of the other actors.

Jorge um brasileiro is the story of a truck driver who is asked to take on an urgent and dangerous assignment. Based on the novel of the same title by Oswaldo França, Jr., the film follows the problems Jorge has in fulfilling the time schedule for his delivery. This involves considerable ingenuity on Jorge's part because many of the roads have been washed out by heavy rains; the ways in which he resolves the problems and dangers he confronts provide the large-scale action basis of this film, making it rather unusual as a Brazilian product. Although there have been other road films made in Brazil (Jorge Bodansky and Wolf Gauner's *Iracema* [1975], for example, is about a prostitute who follows the truck routes during the construction of the Trans-Amazonian Highway in the 1970s), Thiago's film involves considerably more big-ticket action sequences than most productions can afford. According to the review in *Variety* (April 5–11, 1989), *Jorge* cost $1.5 million; most of the films examined in this study were made for half that amount.

The ideological interest of the film lies in the reasons why Jorge is willing to undertake this special assignment. He and his boss, Mário (played by the American star Dean Stockwell—more on this below), were once fellow truckers, working the Trans-Amazonian Highway together. The film has a number of flashbacks that demonstrate the male bond that exists between them: they were once jailed together for stealing a motor belt they needed; Mário organized a cover-up when Jorge accidentally ran over a man who stepped out in front of his truck; when Jorge's father needed emergency medical attention, Mário helped him to get it. Mário, however, was able to start his own company and to take Jorge on as his lead driver. Jorge's ability to make the delivery on time will result in a lucrative government contract for

Mário, and Jorge is willing to delay a much-needed holiday in order to fulfill the demands of a long-standing friendship. Nevertheless, he comes to discover that Mário is simply using him: the class differences that now separate owner from worker have erased any bonds of loyalty Mário may have had for Jorge, who is devastated when he finds out he has merely been used as a dependable employee. In a defiant plot twist that asserts a resistant role for the working class, Jorge goes to Mário's house in his absence; taking advantage of the loneliness of Mário's abandoned but beautiful wife, he seduces her and then walks out. As he is leaving, Mário arrives. Jorge simply walks past him stonily, thereby indicating that no personal relationship any longer exists between them or that any personal relationship that did exist between them is now mediated by the way in which Jorge has just screwed him through his wife—in, of course, a macho oneupmanship retaliation for the way in which Jorge feels he has been screwed by Mário.

Class relationship is, therefore, central to this film, and the bulk of the action involves the bond that exists between the lead trucker and his men. Despite some setbacks and dissension, they all pull together in an idealized solidarity that makes this film an important entry in a newly redemocratized Brazilian cultural production that allows itself to be optimistic with respect to the possibility of social agency. It is an agency that is underscored not only by the affirmation of working-class solidarity and what the spectator is led to believe is a functioning boss-worker relationship of trust and loyalty, but by the way in which the laborer is able to avenge abuse when he discovers that the relationship is not what it seems to be. *Jorge* is hardly a typical Hollywood sentimentalization of the working class or of class conflict, where, *pace* John Ford's *Grapes of Wrath* (1940) or Elia Kazan's *On the Waterfront* (1954), class conflict either does not exist or is made to seem only apparent and therefore facilely resolvable. The seduction of Mário's wife introduces a hard edge of social realism that undercuts any possible suggestion of interclass harmony. The seduction introduces the troubling issue of the abuse of Mário's wife. While Jorge does not rape her and while it is always possible that she is content to be used by a man whose body she apparently has always lusted after, the spectator witnesses the determined way in which Jorge avails himself of her with no attention whatever to the consequences for her and as though such a form of revenge were value-free.

But what is of primary ideological interest in the film is the showcasing of Jorge and his masculinity and the way in which this masculinity is correlated with the issue of class conflict and revenge. Such a correlation is not without its own specific problems, to the extent that it attaches agency to the sort of masculinity Jorge projects. This attachment implies that other forms of masculinity and nonmasculinity cannot have access to such agency. It is also problematical to the extent that it underscores a specific physical embodiment of masculinity (e.g., the actor Carlos Alberto Ricelli's overdetermined body image) and to the extent that it not only excludes the feminine from such an embodiment, but goes on to place the feminine at the unquestioning disposition of the masculine, whereby the exploitation of the woman is never questioned. And, finally, it is problematical to the extent that the hypermasculine establishes, within the masculine and within the male working class, a naturalized supremacy of leadership.

The visual effect of Jorge's body is an immediately evident feature of the film (on the potential impact of bodies in cinema, see Tasker, *Spectacular Bodies*). Although Brazilian films are as capable as Hollywood productions of casting attractive men and women in starring roles to stimulate a form of visual seduction for what is being represented, the dominance in noncommercial Brazilian filmmaking of a criterion of social realism, especially in the legendary Cinema Novo and its contemporary heirs, means that the protagonist is not routinely stunning in a conventional way. The star of Suzana Amaral's *A hora da estrela,* Marcélia Cartaxo, is most effective precisely because of her homeliness in the film.

Ricelli appears to have been charged with projecting a hypermasculine presence. Larger and better-fed than most members of the Brazilian working class and possessing a body that can only be the result of gym work rather than hard labor, Ricelli's Jorge also dresses differently from his fellow workers in order to set off his body. A tight white T-shirt and hip-hugging jeans constitute gender fetishes in a way in which the grungy dress of the other truckers is not likely to, at least not in terms of the range of sexual tastes a mainstream film like *Jorge* is willing to court. Presumably, such a fetishization of Jorge's dress—and, through it, a highlighting of Jorge's body as a fetish—is meant to appeal in an erotic fashion to the interest of the spectator. Filmmaking under the aegis of compulsory heterosexism always assumes that a conventional attractive star appeals universally to the opposite sex, and it is as much willing to foreground such a presumed universal appeal as it is to suppress any hint of having considered the degree to which such an appeal may also be same-sex in nature. This is so both to the extent that there may be a level of polymorphic sexual seduction in every individual and to the extent to which same-sex appeal is not erotic *tout court*.

But it is also rather engaging and fascinating to the extent that it indicates how most spectators fall far short of the gender model the star embodies: I may gaze on Ricelli's body (and the film forces that gaze unless I choose to walk out of the theater) less out of the relatively circumscribed sense in which the erotic is understood than because I am intrigued by the degree to which it surpasses my own particular embodiment of hegemonic masculinity. Gloria Pires, as Mário's wife, Helena, presumably appreciates Jorge's body in direct sexual terms, which is why she is so apparently willing to be seduced by him, but there is no question that the strength as a leader Jorge projects derives from the way in which his body and his dress stand in marked contrast to those of the men over whom he exercises influence. Quite literally, Jorge's body bulks larger than that of the other characters, and this spatial dominance translates, in an easy semiotic displacement, into social power. I do not mean to exaggerate the features of the Ricelli/Jorge body in terms of some sort of Brazilian male norm—as, for example, Arnold Schwarzenegger and Sylvester Stallone are for American norms. The point is that the main protagonist of *Jorge* is not hypermasculine in terms of whatever a Brazilian norm might be, as the overt correlative of a hegemonic heterosexism, but rather is so in terms of his fellow workers, who betray the verisimilar and unhidden scars and deformations of the historical workplace.

It is clear that Thiago, despite the singularity of Jorge in the specific circumstances in which he is shown, meant him to be interpreted as a model, if not of Brazilian masculinity, then of the social agency that is proper to Brazilian masculinity. If the titles of the film and the novel on which it is based singularize Jorge, they do so with the qualifier of "*um* brasileiro," a syntactic detail that confers on him a Brazilian Everyman status. This status is reinforced by the fact that the film title appears in the basic colors of the Brazilian flag, green and yellow. In a society in which, to counter the French feminist Luce Irigaray's attempt to demonstrate the independence of the feminine from the masculine (*Ce Sexe qui n'est pas un* [This Sex Which Is Not One]), there continues to be only one sex, the masculine, against the hegemonic ideal of which all social constructs are measured, the normalizing image that Jorge portrays must be taken at face value.

Thus, in all of Jorge's major social interactions, his body and his actions are a ground zero against which the others are measured: (1) the loyalty he demonstrates toward Mário and the willingness with which he agrees to accept the latter's request that he take on an urgent assignment, despite how it upsets his personal plans; (2) the efficacy of the arrangements he makes to execute that assignment and the degree of confidence he inspires in the men who work under his guidance; (3) the forthright and manly manner in which he makes love to a woman working in a primitive truck stop (a combination bar, restaurant, and dance hall) and honestly convinces her to accompany him on the road without any hint of deceit or betrayal (indeed, the way in which the woman goes along so readily with Jorge, the result in part of his superior lovemaking skills, can be taken as a model of how the spectator is to accept him as an appropriate colossal masculine model); (4) the uncomplicated determination with which Jorge sets out to avenge Mário's betrayal. Rather than experiencing conflicting sentiments or an ambiguous decision, Jorge seduces Mário's wife in the same take-charge manner in which he saves his former friend's cargo. Jorge's body is one of the "spectacular bodies" that Yvonne Tasker analyzes in Hollywood films. Her phrase does not mean that these bodies are spectacular in the sense of being overwhelming. Rather, they are display texts, bodies as spectacle, bodies invested with an overdetermined meaning that allows them to function as the semiotic point of reference for the filmic text.

The very fact that this seduction is without problems from his point of view and presumably does not matter from the woman's point of view serves to underscore how what does matter is Jorge's social conduct and the example he is meant to embody. Certainly, all cultural products are cultural allegories, in the sense that ideological values are at play in the exposition of a particular plot, no matter how much it may be based on allegedly unique human characters. This is especially so if a product is read, or suggests that it be read, against the backdrop of a sociohistorical context, in accord with the principles of film interpretation proposed by Masud Zavarzadeh in his *Seeing Films Politically*. In the case of *Jorge um brasileiro*, made during the period of redemocratization and involving a business deal between a private citizen and a constitutional government, the ideological context is difficult to avoid. And as I have insisted, the title itself provides an opening to a specifically allegorical interpretation based on the Everyman generalization of the indefinite/unspecific pronoun.

Thiago's film is particularly noteworthy because of the presence of Dean Stockwell (his voice is dubbed by Odilon Wagner). In the first place, Stockwell has worked in a number of U.S. films well known to Latin American movie connoisseurs, such as David Lynch's *Blue Velvet* (1986). The fact that he is not just another inconsequential actor demands that some ideological importance be attached to his presence in this film. U.S. films have long used foreign actors to provide a dimension of exoticism, and the use of Stockwell (as well as the sound processing, done in the United States by Dolby—sound has traditionally been notoriously problematical for Brazilian and other Latin American filmmaking) may well have been Thiago's gesture in this direction.

Whatever the basis of Thiago's use of Stockwell is, his presence opens up another useful line of inquiry in an ideological interpretation of the film: the way in which the foreign actor adds a marked difference to the construction of the character he represents. Mário is as Brazilian as Jorge. However, he belongs to a different social domain, first by virtue of his having become the owner-boss and second by having become a son-of-a-bitch against whom Jorge's masculine authenticity defines itself. Since Stockwell is not Brazilian, he neither looks Brazilian nor, more importantly, handles his body as a Brazilian does. This does not mean that

Stockwell is incapable of communicating with his body. It only means that the way in which he handles his body is that of an American man and actor. Thiago seems not to have been interested in getting Stockwell to look and act Brazilian (except for having his voice dubbed by a native speaker of Brazilian Portuguese); I would like to assume that, as a director, Thiago was conscious of what the advantages of Stockwell's not being Brazilian could be for the parameters of meaning in the film.

Stockwell's subliminal difference (of course, most spectators would be aware of the fact that a non-Brazilian is playing the role) adds a dimension of sinister otherness to Mário's character. In this way, he does not have to play Mário as sinister, which would have given the film a superficial quality. All he has to do is play Mário as a rather indifferent boss who knows he can count on Jorge's loyalty. The difference in body between the two men— Ricelli is muscular, while Stockwell is sinewy—and the difference in body language—Ricelli's controlled extroversion vs. Stockwell's detached, at times almost vacant, inwardness—is enough to establish a significant distance between their two characters that turns out to be charged with significance when we discover that Jorge has been duped by Mário. Moreover, at the conclusion of the film, when the two men cross in the street in front of Mário's house, the masculine dignity of Jorge contrasts with the well-dressed insignificance of Mário: the spectator is supposed to have no reason for investing any sympathy in the latter.

It is a more open question whether Stockwell's presence in the film has another subliminal dimension to it: that of the U.S.A. vs. Brazil. A recurrent theme during the resistance to twenty years of neofascist dictatorship in Brazil was the supporting hand of the United States and its avowed opposition to the spread of communism in Brazil. After the return to constitutional institutionalism in 1985, and especially with the neoliberalist project of recent years, the ground has shifted to U.S. economic interests and the restructuring of Brazil's national economy to support and defend them. This defense has enormous implications, since neoliberalism in Latin America is designed principally to provide some recovery of the internal debt; constitutional continuity is important only to the extent that it favors that recovery by providing a context more propitious for widespread economic penetration than the military dictatorships proved to be. The fact that Mário is the devious boss, willing to exploit a past comradeship, even if it means putting his lead trucker in considerable danger from natural elements and police authority, cannot be overlooked, and his otherness in the work is fundamentally based on the fact that he is an American actor.

The hypermasculinity of Thiago's Jorge, grounded as it is in a complex code of heterosexist hegemony, which includes male supremacy and female marginalization and dependency, ends up lending this film an overbearing allegorical quality. It provides a strident model for something like a Brazilian New Man during the early years of the dictatorship. Significantly, that New Man will not overcome in any facile, and therefore inconsequential, way the forces of oppression that exist in any society that has had a long period of military dictatorship, with the social, political, and economic devastation that such a circumstance brings. The important point of *Jorge um brasileiro* that is made via the codes of masculinity Ricelli articulates is a measure of male social agency, such that, without police consequences, Jorge may, as the Johnny Paycheck song goes, tell Mário to "take this job and shove it."

The world of truck drivers in Brazil is an exclusively masculine one, and the homosocial bonding that exists between these knights of the highway gives them a strength of presence that they cannot have as individuals. Brazil travels by highway, and most of the goods of the country move by long-distance supertrucks, which also endows the men with a specific social signification. As one of the characters says at one point: "Estrada é coisa para homem" (The highway is for men). Thiago's film is valuable for the modeling of social agency for the working man after two decades in which such agency existed solely for those allied with military power. But this is so only if one can look beyond the antifeminism inherent in the homosociality of the trucker reality depicted, something that is even more evident in França's novel, which is narrated in the first person. Such a narrative positioning serves to focus on the male protagonist, his seduction of Mário's wife, and his hypermasculinity, which almost threatens at times to become a caricature of itself.

Lamarca

When the army was finally successful in hunting down Carlos Lamarca and murdering him on September 17, 1971, as he lay weakened from malaria in a small village in the outback, he had become one of the most notorious revolutionary leaders of the urban guerrilla movement in Brazil to protest the dictatorship imposed by the 1964 military coup. Guerrilla movements in Brazil, both urban and rural, were implacably crushed by the military in concert (often with direct international collaboration) with the armed forces of the other Latin American countries that were experiencing neofascist tyranny and its concomitant armed resistance: Bolivia, Uruguay, Argentina, Chile.

What was particularly iconic about Lamarca, however, was the fact that he was a highly respected and extensively decorated military officer—he had recently been promoted to major—who switched his allegiance to the guerrilla cause. Lamarca had served with a Brazilian expeditionary force in the Suez Canal, and it has been claimed that it was the perspective of that international experience, including the sight of the suffering of indigenous peoples in Africa at the hands of the colonial empires, that enabled him to understand how the poverty and injustice in Brazil were not just a local circumstance but part of the system of global capitalism. Institutional armed forces were the enforcers of this system, and the Brazilian armed forces were, in effect, an expeditionary force, an occupying army—especially with their visibility as part of the enforcement of the *linha dura* (hard line)—in their own country.

Lamarca's defection was an acute embarrassment to the Brazilian military, and there could never be any question of allowing him to get away with such an outrage, such an affront to institutional honor. As the officer in charge of hunting him down says to a police agent in charge of antiterrorism, only a military man can understand another military man's mentality, and it is the military's responsibility to liquidate Lamarca. Although the record of the guerrilla movement in Latin America reveals cases of close family members of military officers who fought with the guerrilla opposition (for example, a niece of the Argentine governing junta in the 1970s, General Emilio Massera, was a guerrilla member, as were the sons and daughters of various other generals—see Moyano, *Argentina's Lost Patrol,* 164), Lamarca was unusual in being the only known case during the period of a high-ranking official who betrayed his oath of allegiance to fight with the guerrillas. The fact that Lamarca was engaged in insurgency operations for only a little over a year indicates the grim determination with which the military pursued him with the goal of exterminating this particularly outrageous blot on their institutional honor. If the rhetoric of the Latin American military in its persecution of armed resistance made enraged use of terms like "foreign agents," "traitors to the fatherland," and "subversive scum," they paled by comparison to the interpretation of Lamarca's betrayal.

Rezende's film, released in 1994, while it does dwell on some of the problematical aspects of the guerrilla movement, is unqualified in its martyrological, indeed, even Christological, interpretation of Lamarca (who, as is pointed out in the film, was thirty-three at the time of his murder). It casts him virtually on a par with the Argentine Ernesto (Che) Guevara, who is the chief icon of the guerrilla operative made sacrificial victim (cf. his *El diario del Che en Bolivia*). This is accomplished in large measure by using Paulo Betti in the lead role. Betti looks very much like Lamarca, as can be determined from the pictures in Emiliano José and Oldack Miranda's book, *Lamarca: O capitão da guerrilha* (1980), on which Rezende's film is based. Betti has a cultivated sheen that enhances Lamarca's image considerably, especially as he is juxtaposed throughout the movie with actors who do not have the same degree of ad-agency masculinity that Betti exudes. In addition to his well-exercised body (the film acknowledges the contribution of a professional athletic trainer), his chiseled features and the full sensuousness of his sharply defined lips provide Betti's Lamarca with a seductive sexual allure that is typical of the traditional Hollywood star. That allure is meant to appeal to a heterosexual audience on the basis of presumed male fantasies of the female spectator and the desire for convincing models—refinedly hypermasculine without being "pretty"—for the male spectator; audience members with alternative sexual preferences reconstruct this scheme as necessary.

One does not wish to overgeneralize about the construction

LAMARCA
O filme de Sergio Rezende acompanha os dois últimos anos da vida do Capitão Carlos Lamarca (Paulo Betti), desde o momento em que, casado com Marina (Deborah Evelin), decide fazer uma opção radical pela revolução enviando a mulher e os dois filhos para Cuba e desertando do Exército em janeiro de 1969, até sua morte em 1971. Na clandestinidade, ligado a Vanguarda Popular Revolucionária (VPR), Lamarca comanda assaltos e seqüestros, apaixona-se por Clara (Carla Camurati) e amadurece em suas convicções políticas. Começa a sofrer, também, a perseguição sem trégua do delegado Flores (Ernani Moraes), e depois do Exército, sob o comando de um Major (José de Abreu) determinado a derrotar a qualquer preço "o traidor da bandeira".
ANO DE PRODUÇÃO 1994
Produção Morena Filmes e Cinema Filmes com
TEMPO DE DURAÇÃO 130 MIM.
Paulo Betti, Carla Camurati,
José de Abreu, Deborah Evelin, Eliezer de Almeida, Ernani Morais, Roberto Bomtempo.
Roteiro Sergio Rezende e Alfredo Oróz
Fotografia Antonio Luiz Mendes
Música David Tygel
Montagem Isabelle Rathery
Direção de Arte Clóvis Bueno
Figurinos Rita Murtinho
Uma Produção José Joffily e Mariza Leão
PATROCINIO
banespa
RIOFILME
SAGRES
DRAMA
NTSC-VHS
107/94
LAMARCA
RIOFILME
SAGRES
MARIZA LEÃO APRESENTA UM FILME DE SERGIO REZENDE
LAMARCA
UMA HISTÓRIA NÃO CONTADA DOS ANOS REBELDES
Paulo Betti
Carla Camurati
José de Abreu. Deborah Evelin
RIOFILME
SAGRES

Video promotion for ***Lamarca.***
Reproduced by permission of Sagres Home Video Ltd.

of audience identification. But, of course, this is precisely what happens from the point of view of cinematographic production: there is every reason to believe that production considerations involve an appeal to a particular type of spectator, which is an integral part of the particular message a film, as a cultural text, has to transmit. Whether or not this takes place and whether or not specific spectators, with their undeterminable reactions and their uncontainable ideological formations, react as expected is something else again. But part of the success of a film is the ability to reach a specific spectator, ultimately cast in terms of a large-based audience, and it is reasonable for filmic analysis to consider what that audience might be like and what they might find important in the story of a by now relatively obscure guerrilla leader murdered twenty-five years ago during the height of a harsh military dictatorship most Brazilians would prefer to forget.

It is clear that Rezende wishes to resuscitate the figure of Lamarca, which was also the goal of José and Miranda. There is no longer any threat of armed revolution in Brazil, where the greatest menace now comes from armed criminal activity and assault at the hands of the economically desperate and where the state uses the concept of a war against drugs as a way to keep the poor under control: the police only attack and terrorize the *favelas* (slums), never the high-rises. For this reason, it is now possible to revisit figures like Lamarca with some measure of historical objectivity, indeed, even to make a film like *Lamarca* with what appears to be a measure of assistance of the armed forces for the military scenes: although the film may have been made without such assistance, the very fact that it appears to be present is significant. Fully conscious that there is little sense in romanticizing Lamarca—the legacy of Che Guevara has little reason to fear Brazilian competition—Rezende does, nevertheless, have a clear agenda with regard to explaining the motivations and the consequences of Lamarca's decision to commit himself fully to the cause of armed revolution.

In pursuing this goal, Rezende has three fundamental problems to resolve. First, he must appeal to an audience who for the most part have no idea of who Lamarca was or only remember him sketchily—theater audiences in Brazil tend to be composed of people under thirty, so historical memory becomes an immediate issue. Second, he must defend the principles of armed revolution in a society in which, unlike the case in Argentina, the dictatorship essentially succeeded (or essentially succeeded in supporting the proposition that it had succeeded) and in which the transition to institutional democracy in 1985 was to be viewed as a component of that success. Third, he must defend an individual who betrayed his military rank, not because there is any driving promilitary stance in Brazil, but because of the overdetermined way in which Lamarca's subversion of patriotic institutions from within was to any degree successful in portraying him as a villain at the time and subsequently suppressing him from history.

In order to make Lamarca attractive to what may be viewed

as an initially cold audience with perhaps only a passing interest in revisiting a history more than two decades old, Rezende's first major strategy is to rely on Betti to bear the heavy weight of making Lamarca a convincing and commanding masculine presence within certain conventions of heterosexist society. Thus, Betti's striking physical presence must be complemented by a series of features in terms of behavior and attitude that maintain him always as a magnetic center of the picture. Although this in part means filming Lamarca as always, quite literally, the center of every frame in which he appears, in the larger terms of the construction of meaning it entails organizing each narrative segment so that his intervention may be seen as positive, as a contribution toward confirming the symbolic value of his person.

Thus, for example, in those sequences dealing with guerrilla activity, he is a measuredly confident agent of the group's activities. He is able to take charge, to weigh personal and political factors, to assess the potential and the limitations of those working with him, to speak convincingly and to react sincerely, and always to confirm the importance for the armed revolution of having inherited a leader trained by the armed forces against which they are struggling. The film ends up trivializing Lamarca because he is seen as virtually flawless in his execution of the guerrilla paradigm, and his "purity" in this regard casts him in the role of a mythified and highly personalized caudillo, which undermines his meaning in terms of the social revolutionary ideology of the period.

This becomes almost comical when, in an intimate scene with Clara, a colleague who is pretending to be his wife in order to hide how their apartment is a center of guerrilla operations, Lamarca draws back from her erotic advances, claiming that he is a married man and a father. He has sent his wife and children to Cuba to protect them, and numerous flashbacks throughout the film confirm their importance in his life. Lamarca's wife reacts strongly against his decision to turn traitor, alleging that his family is more important than political convictions. However, she reluctantly accedes to his plan, while continuing to lament leaving him behind while she and the children depart for Cuba. Clara here is, in reality, Iara (Iavelberg) Haberkorn. The historical Iara committed suicide, as does Clara in the movie, in August 1971 after being cornered in the building in which she lived with Lamarca in Bahia. Rezende, by rather transparently changing Iara's identity, may have wished to suppress the erotic relationship that existed between the two; of course, he could also have been gesturing toward the common practice whereby participants in the armed struggle frequently went under assumed names (see the book on Iara by Judith Lieblich Patarra, *Iara: Reportagem biográfica*).

The most important way in which Lamarca is idealized is in the second half of the film, which details his attempts to elude pursuit by the military in the Bahia outback. There are four components to this representation. The first involves Lamarca's refuge in the desert, where he meditates on his mission, his family, and his fortune in the fashion of Christ alone in Gethsemane. The figure of Lamarca, in all his sober masculinity, cast against the backdrop of the wasteland signifies his struggle against the impossible odds of social injustice in Brazil; his determination to survive, as he writes letters to his loved ones, performs calisthenics to keep in shape, and assesses his strategy, parallels his determination for his cause to prevail. The second component involves interactions with his supporters from the nearby town of Buriti Cristalino, who essentially venerate him, according him full military deference, which only means that they will end up suffering the same martyrdom meted out to Lamarca.

Concomitantly, when Lamarca and Zequinha (his principal companion in Buriti Cristalino, who will die alongside him) stop in the town of Pintada, where the military will eventually catch up with him after one peasant betrays them in Judas-like fashion, another, a young woman (inspired by Lamarca's virility?), warns them of the betrayal in an admirable gesture of solidarity. Finally, there are the Christological dimensions of Lamarca's death. Rezende dramatically changes the actual facts: Lamarca, already seriously ill from his ordeal in the outback, was found with his head resting on a flat stone (see the photograph on p. 180 of the José and Miranda book). Rezende has him die with his arms fully extended over a piece of wood in an obvious reference to Calvary. Needless to say, the circumstances of Lamarca's death are contrasted with the viciousness of the military patrol's leader, who in cross-cut sequences mutters incessantly about Lamarca's perfidy and continues to fire into his body even when it is clear that he is dead.

Rezende's appeal to his audience in support of Lamarca, in addition to Betti's formidable virility and exemplary masculinity, depends to a great extent on the calculation of an antimilitary sentiment on the part of the audience. It would be no exaggeration to say that the Brazilian military, thanks to a dictatorship that lasted over two decades, does not count on a large reservoir of enthusiastic public support, although it is clear that for someone like Lamarca, from a solid petit-bourgeois background, a military career constituted an enormous opportunity for social advancement. But the difference between the career opportunities of the military for specific individuals and its overall social profile is immense; if Brazilians are not virulently antimilitaristic, there is no reason to believe that there can be much sympathy for the institution Lamarca became a turncoat to, at least not as Rezende portrays it in his film.

In large measure, the interest of *Lamarca* is based on the opposition between two armed forces, the institutional army and the guerrilla movement. In the fairly extensive cultural production in Latin America on armed resistance in the 1960s and 1970s, the guerrilla movement is pitted against the state, which happens to be militarized in the form of a military dictatorship (the most famous document describing this resistance, a document colored by the failure that cuts it short, is the diary of Che Guevara's disastrous campaign in Bolivia in the mid-1960s). However, in this case, the armed forces are an instrument of the state, and the story to be told is the eternal one of the individual vs. the state, a story as old as Greek tragedy. As such, the instrument of the armed forces is depersonalized because it is subsumed under a larger entity that is cloaked in the multiple facets of the ideology of the state, with its themes of patriotism, national identity, and abiding superstructures.

In Rezende's film the state is superseded by the army: it is not the armed forces as a corporate conglomerate, but one specific agency, the army. The armed forces have become the state, and to question the armed forces is to question the state, to engage in an unpatriotic challenge to the *pátria amada* (the beloved fatherland—note the gendering here). Indeed, this is the period in which the bumpersticker emerges: "O Brasil, ame-o o deixe-o" (Brazil, love it or leave it). Thus, in the initial presentation of guerrilla operations, repression is shown to be in the hands of the police, and the spectator is reminded of the patterns of persecution, entrapment, wholesale searches and arrests, and torture, with the goal of extracting information that will initiate the process all over again. The film returns to the representation of police operations when it shows, while Lamarca is enduring his solitary retreat in the outback, the operation that leads to the entrapment and suicide of Clara (Iara). Nevertheless, when it becomes a question of tracking Lamarca down for his guerrilla activities, the army informs the police officer in charge that it is an army matter and that the army will assume the responsibility in the operation against Lamarca.

Significantly, that operation does not turn on capturing/torturing/executing Lamarca for his guerrilla activities, but rather on avenging the insult he handed the army by putting his military training at the service of the armed resistance. In this way, the pursuit of Lamarca is personalized in a way that the police operation against the essentially anonymous, "masked" guerrillas is not. The guerrillas are viewed as an underidentified mass, and it is their extermination as a group (an interpretation furthered by the metaphors of denunciation by the police: animals, vermin, subversive hoards, and the like) that is the goal of the apparatus of repression. Lamarca, by contrast, is highlighted as an individual, *the one* army officer to betray his uniform, *the one* to make the transition from army captain to guerrilla captain.

If Lamarca is individuated in an exceptional way, the army's pursuit of him is too, in the person of Major Cerqueira, who leads the "Operação Cão" against Lamarca. The final segment of the film moves back and forth between scenes of Cerqueira's pursuit and scenes of Lamarca's increasingly futile attempt to evade capture. This alternation underscores how this has become a personal vendetta rather than an operation by the state. Film has customarily found it necessary to personalize in this way: Brechtian distancing and epic narrative seek to avoid the personalization of history so integral to bourgeois culture, but it is this sort of personalization, which is virtually synonymous with mass-audience filmmaking, that Rezende depends on for the rhetorical structure of his film. For this reason, when Cerqueira and Lamarca come face to face, Cerqueira simply murders him: capture, court-martial, imprisonment, execution have nothing to do with the vengeance the army has charged Cerqueira with seeking. Thus, it is with the image of Lamarca's bullet-riddled corpse that the film must end, since there can be no history subsequent to the execution of personalized revenge.

In this way, Rezende has constructed his film as personal biography, and in this way he is able to heroize Lamarca by villainizing Cerqueira, which he does both by the fashion in which Cerqueira's character is enacted and by the historical facts surrounding the torture and murder of individuals in Buriti Cristalino in order to determine Lamarca's whereabouts. To this extent, then, Rezende does not really have to pursue beyond superficial images the history of the military dictatorship, guerrilla operations, and police/military persecutions, much less the position of "ordinary" citizens and their relationship to and understanding of the Brazilian social history in the 1960s and 1970s. The spectators as figures of those so-called ordinary citizens (or so they are presumed to be, since it is not evident that films are seen in Brazil by a true cross-section of society) are spared having to engage in an interpretation of dictators and guerrillas. Rather, they are asked only to invest in the human superiority of Lamarca, an investment facilitated both by the villainy of his pursuers and by the idealization of his character, abetted by Betti's hypermasculinity.

Yet what must inevitably happen is that by rhetorically overcharging the representation of Lamarca's personal story, Rezende's film cannot mean (as any other interpretive consequence) the vindication, if not of the guerrilla movement, then of an individual guerrilla commitment as an outstanding human being. Unlike Constantin Costa-Gavras's *State of Siege* (1973), on the Uruguayan Tupamaro urban guerrilla movement, where no personalization takes place (except, for reasons of historical accuracy, in Yves Montagne's muted role as the kidnapped American

Agency for International Development officer) and where there is an attempt to analyze critically the issues of armed resistance in the context of a brutal military dictatorship with all of the weight of Washington behind it, *Lamarca* has no interest in historical assessment. It remains from beginning to end Betti's strong masculine enactment of a personal, tragic odyssey that ends up proposing to the spectator an alluring figure of a guerrilla martyr.

Ópera do malandro

Despite the way in which society tends to believe that major social constructs like masculinity are universal and timeless, the historical record shows major shifts, if not in the overall construction of gender identity, at least in significant details relating to it. Certainly, a type of feminist proposal that, rather than questioning the gender binary, asks men to get in touch with their feminine side is, for American society, the demand for a significant departure from the paradigm of a masculinity predicated on the detailed and wholesale repudiation of anything that can be associated with the feminine. The legitimation of homoeroticism in any of its meanings and the defense of bisexuality cannot, likewise, be accommodated in such a paradigm, nor is it possible to envision any assimilation of the masculine by what is considered to be a properly feminine (= the absence of the masculine as dominant) paradigm.

Brazil is a society that is no less absolute than any other in holding onto a fixed paradigm of masculinity, one in which deviations that are tolerated and even accepted only serve to reinforce the primacy of the dominant scheme of things sexual (see Dollimore, *Sexual Dissidence*). Yet Rui Guerra's *Ópera do malandro* (1986) constitutes an excellent example of a paradigm shift in the definition of the masculine in contemporary Brazilian filmmaking. The movie version of Chico Buarque [de Hollanda]'s 1978 play of the same name, whose published text contains the subtitle *Comédia musical,* is superficially a Brazilian attempt to execute a Hollywood-style musical. Buarque's text is a Brazilian version in the tradition of the same sources as John Gay's 1728 *Beggar's Opera,* Bertolt Brecht's 1928 *The Threepenny Opera,* and Menahem Golan's 1989 movie *Mack the Knife,* starring Raúl Juliá (see also Rubén Blades's own version of this material, "Pedro Navaja").

Guerra's movie, however, is a much-simplified version of Buarque's play. Not only are approximately half of the dozen or so songs of the stage play used in the movie, but the time (well) spent on developing visual images in the film detracts from the opportunity to deal with all of the plot details of the play. This is undoubtedly common in the translation of plays, with a much different theatrical language, into the language of film, and the point here is to discuss *Ópera do malandro* as a film and not merely as a recorded version of the play. Guerra certainly captures the sense of Buarque's play: the transition from the primitive individual capitalism of traditional premodern Brazilian culture in which social, political, and police structures exist to enhance isolated capital accumulation and exploitation based on the law of the jungle to complex modern investment capitalism that relies on an organized infrastructure and a formal system that transcends the individual player—the former is personalist, while the latter is institutional in nature.

Played out against the combined backdrop of the Getúlio Vargas fascist-inspired Estado Novo and the Second World War (specifically, events are set in 1941–1942), *Ópera do malandro* tells the story of Max Overseas, a small-time crook and pimp who is clever enough first to get involved in the selling of consumer goods smuggled into Brazil by American sailors on boats that dock in Rio de Janeiro as part of the growing importance of Latin America to the war effort in the Atlantic and, second, to transfer his erotic allegiance from Marlene, a prostitute who works out of the Hamburgo cabaret, to Ludmila, the convent-bred daughter of the German Nazi sympathizer Otto Strudel, who owns the Hamburgo. This transfer of allegiance allows Max to tap into the money Ludmila wheedles out of her father to pursue her own business interests. Strudel at first resists her alliance with Max, a man whom he considers beneath the social aspirations he and his former prostitute wife have for the daughter they have paid so much to raise as a respectable woman. But the German abandons his opposition to the Americans in order to back his daughter and

Max, who will take advantage of the growing relations between Brazil and the United States to establish what has all the appearance of being the precursor of a multinational conglomerate. In the process, "artisanal" corruption has been replaced by a slick entrepreneurial society.

Like the textual tradition in which Guerra's film participates, the *malandro* is viewed fundamentally not as a marginal social phenomenon, an outlaw who functions in the mostly hidden underworld of a social life that would be all the better for his disappearance. Rather, the *malandro* is a foot soldier (one of the early scenes of the film involves the choreographed dance of a platoon of *malandros,* all dressed in the same uniform) of the economic system, a highly efficient agent of the interplay of corruption, influence peddling, payoffs, exploitation, and strong-arm control that is the very essence of patriarchal capitalism. It matters little whether that capitalism assumes the primitive rough-hewn jungle forms of the Hamburgo and environs or whether it takes on the glossy form of Lu and Max enterprises—or, for that matter, whether it evolves into the neoliberal enterprise ventures that, when Guerra's film was made, already obviously lay in the cards for Brazil in its transition from military dictatorship to institutional democracy (supported by the United States and its commercial interests, which had come to understand that democracy rather than tyranny would, in the long run, be better for business).

Ópera do malandro in either guise, as theater or as film, is an excellent example of a Marxian economic analysis translated into a cultural text. Guerra preserves in his film the way in which Buarque wishes to demonstrate how social configurations are driven by economic considerations and how changes in the economic structure affect superstructural matters such as interpersonal relationships, value beliefs, and social institutions. The plot turns on a central issue of human relations—erotic liaisons—and it culminates in two major social institutions that are viewed as continuous with each other—marriage and business partnerships. In the transition from one economic system to the other, from primitive profiteering to capitalist enterprise, the valences of the elements that make up these structural phenomena shift.

Max Overseas is loved by the cabaret star and prostitute

Marlene (he is also loved by the transvestite star Geni, and this forms a homoerotic subtheme of the movie). Marlene is a woman of the streets, and Max in part lives off her earnings ("There is nothing like a woman's money," he says at one point). She is savvy and tough, as the law of survival dictates, and she is able to alternate her passion for Max with outbursts of violent rage when she thinks he has done her wrong. Max, fulfilling a law of prostitute narratives, does do her wrong: he falls in love with Ludmila. Ludmila is as savvy and tough as Marlene is, although, of course, her wiles are enveloped in the silk and lace of a convent-bred *senhorita*. But she also knows how to take care of herself out in the world, and she has no intention of letting Marlene get in the way or of allowing Max to dominate her. When she first gives him money to invest for her, she tells him to sign a blank receipt; she'll fill in the amount later herself.

There are three big dance sequences in the film. The first is the aforementioned parade of the platoon of *malandros* in the street at night; the second is at Max and Ludmila's wedding (more on this below). The third is a duel between Marlene and Ludmila. While it is clear that Ludmila will win the choreographed confrontation between the two women, what holds the spectator's attention is how it is a dance of equals, with Ludmila able to match and better every one of Marlene's erotic moves, gestures, and poses: Ludmila comes down to Marlene's level, so to speak, in displaying a completely sexualized body, so that the pretenses of her convent upbringing drop away as completely irrelevant to her personal agenda. Marlene comes up to Ludmila's level (but not enough to best her) by showing that she is a match for Ludmila and that she is not simply willing to disappear because a social better has challenged her place in Max's life.

Ludmila does get Max, both as a husband and as a business partner, but the process points up the change in economic structures in Brazil. When Ludmila insists on marrying Max as part of the business arrangement between the two, her father goes into a rage: he has other ideas for his daughter's social station. He enlists the aid of the corrupt police officer Tigrão to scare Max off. Tigrão and Max grew up together, and the confrontation between the two of them at the beginning of the film, with the former dressed in black and the latter in white, is also a sort of duel that neither wins at that moment between two sides of the same coin of the social system: the outlaw and the corrupt lawman. The way in which Max will prevail over Tigrão is prefigured in this early confrontation: when Tigrão draws out his gun, Max makes fun of it as a museum piece, as he draws out his own shining gun, one of his many contraband purchases from the busy U.S. seamen. The homoerotic content of this confrontation is eloquent: they meet in a men's room, challenge each other as they urinate into facing urinals, and show each other their "guns." Tigrão, when he goes to threaten Max, rather than kill him, kills Geni. Although Tigrão forces Max to leave Brazil for Argentina and takes over his operations, Max will soon return to assert his proprietorship. In the process, he will, in a symbolic castration, strip Tigrão of his pants and mark his face with a razor. The latter is as much a paradigmatic assertion of masculine preeminence as the former is a metonymy of anal rape.

Tigrão shows up at Max and Ludmila's wedding as an emissary of her father, who is at first determined to separate the two. Although his ostensible, and presumably honest, reason is to prevent his daughter from being "wasted" on Max, he is equally concerned about the challenge to his business interests represented by Max and his daughter's operations. But when Max returns from Argentina and humiliates Tigrão, which takes place at about the same time that Brazil declares its opposition to Nazi Germany and threatens to confiscate German holdings in the country while at the same time declaring itself for the U.S. war effort, Otto finds that it is to his advantage to ally himself with Max and his daughter. The play closes with a reprise of the wedding/consolidation of the business partnership, with Otto proudly toasting his daughter and new son-in-law and his new commercial partners.

A wedding is of paramount personal and social importance. Much more than marking an important passage for a couple that will, it is believed, give definitive meaning to their lives, it also marks their triumphant incorporation into the dominant institution of the patriarchy and the confirmation of the code of compulsory heterosexuality. Although this incorporation may be in part ironic in *Ópera do malandro,* to the extent that it is not clear that happy family life is what Ludmila and Max have in mind, it is certainly a normalization of erotic love that stands in marked opposition to the domain of prostitution that Marlene stands for. Yet, if business and matrimony are two sides of the same coin of the patriarchy—in the sense that, beyond the concept of marrying for reasons of financial alliance or viewing the family unit as the essential commercial marketplace, business requires the stability and regularization of life that matrimony is claimed to provide— Ludmila's insistence on marriage and her father's fulsome toast at the conclusion of the film underscore the continuity between the two institutions. *Ópera do malandro* is not just a love story about people with business interests; nor is it the story of a commercial venture that happens to have a love story attached to it. It is about fundamental social institutions that are involved in and serve economic structures, such that the individual's personal erotic history can only be understood in the context of hegemonic social institutions that define and shape it.

Ópera do malandro is, as befits a Marxian analysis, overdeterminedly contextualized historically. The factual backdrop of the movie is the conflict that emerges in Brazil over the support of Germany vs. the support of the United States. Brazil's official decision in early 1942 to support the Allies, despite deep German roots in the country and the fact that President Getúlio Vargas's Estado Novo government rested solidly on fascist principles, constituted a veritable sea change. U.S. interests were already strong in the country; as part of U.S. Atlantic commerce, merchant marines had long had Rio de Janeiro as a port of call, and they were joined by the naval fleet. Indeed, it is from U.S. seamen (it is not very clear in the movie whether they are sailors or merchant marines) that Max purchases his contraband wares, the key one being his modern U.S. service pistol. Brazil's decision to support the United States is, at the time, a strategic political one, but it is also a gamble on who will win the war. The U.S. victory in World War II not only confirms the dismantling of German commercial interests in Brazil, but also seriously undermines those of France and Britain, opening the door for what will be the dominance of the Brazilian economy for the rest of the century (through U.S. dominance will also, of course, come Japanese dominance, based in part on the incursion of Japanese interests in the country that had begun after World War I).

In the concluding scene of the movie, as Max is toasted by his father-in-law, he leads his associates in a dance of celebration, strutting around in a blue suit with a red handkerchief stuck in the pocket and a white shirt (replacing, significantly, the Nazi-style black shirt worn with a white suit that is his uniform as a *malandro*). The American epoch has been inaugurated in Brazilian business.[2] In Buarque's play, this final confirmation merits the longest and most spectacular number of the play, and it is a pity it was not incorporated into the film:

JOÃO ALEGRE [= Otto in the film]
> *Telegrama*
> *Do Alabama*
> *Pro senhor Max*
> *Overseas*
> *Ai, meu Deus do céu*
> *Me sinto tão feliz*

TERESINHA [= Ludmila in the film]
> *Chegou a confirmação*
> *Da United coisa e tal*
> *Que nos passa a conçessão*
> *Para o náilon tropical*

MAX
> *Então nós vamos montar*
> *Em São Paulo um fabricão*

TERESINHA
> *Depois vamos exportar*
> *Fio de náilon pro Japão*

MAX
> *Sei que o náilon tem valor*
> *Mas começa a me enjoar*
> *Tive idéia bem melhor*
> *Nós vamos ramificar*

TERESINHA
> *Já ramifiquei, ha ha*
> *Fiz acordo com a Shell*

Coca-Cola, RCA
E vai ser sopa no mel
CORO
Que beleza
Que riqueza
Tá chovendo
Da matriz
Ai, meu Deus do céu
Me sinto tão feliz. (182)[3]

The transition in Max's masculinity is as dramatic as the change in his social and economic condition. In the first place, he renounces the alley-cat life he has led as a *malandro* and as a *cafetão* (pimp). He may continue to live off a woman, but it will be his legitimate wife and business partner. This normalization of Max's erotic life also involves the elimination of what else might be problematical in his erotic history, specifically the transvestite Geni (he claims to love Max, but there is never any indication of sexual relations between the two men, although the pansexuality of the *malandro,* who can command whatever partner he wishes, is legendary) and the childhood friend and rival, Tigrão. In this way, Max is thoroughly heterosexualized, and it is clear that Ludmila will in no way allow him to be anything other than a dutiful helpmate: she would be quite capable of castrating him were she ever to catch him with Marlene again. Finally, through his association with Ludmila, Max is not only normalized by heterosexual matrimony, but is also converted into a paradigmatic U.S. businessman, as characterized by his dressing in the colors of the American flag.

Although it may be an open question as to exactly what all this means, Max's Americanization stands in vivid contrast to his Brazilian persona as a quintessential *malandro*. It is likely that nothing much will change in terms of the corruption, exploitation, and intimidation of the marketplace. But Max has changed dramatically, as a man and as a businessman, and the change in the construction of his masculinity signals the profound changes in Brazilian society that will come with the new American ways of doing business: as everyone says, "Ai, meu Deus do céu / Me sinto tão feliz."

O boto

One of the principal elements of the masculinist, heterosexist construction of femininity is that of the woman out of control. This construction may be expressed in the broad terms of all women as the temptress daughters of Eve (a motif more trenchantly formulated in terms of woman as quintessentially a slut) or in the formulations of female hysteria that are essential to Freudianism and the tradition of the medicalization of women's psychology that it has inspired. In either case, woman is viewed as a victim of her immutable nature. It is the duty of patriarchal men not only to protect themselves against this nature, but to protect women against themselves, which is only another way of protecting the patriarchy from the allegedly dire consequences of woman's lust and its correlative, woman's anger in the face of lust frustrated. Feminist theoreticians like Mary Daly, far from repudiating an acute and singularly female emotionalism as more establishment feminists have found it urgent to do, have attempted to capitalize on the belief in such emotionalism and to promote the proposition that it is only through its intensive and purposeful cultivation and its distillation in *Pure Lust,* as one of Daly's titles announces, that woman will be definitively free of the destructive hand of the patriarchy. For both mainline feminists and radical feminists like Mary Daly, any suggestion of the "innate" lustfulness of women—at least, of a lustfulness that exceeds that of men and renders women incapable of exercising the control over their own lives that men have—is an appallingly retrograde formulation of women's lives.

However, this is exactly what Walter Lima Júnior's 1987 film *O boto* does in fact formulate. Apparently meant to be an enchanting and lyric evocation of erotic sensuality (at least according to the text on the video cassette box of its U.S. release), Lima's film, which is based on Amazonian legendary material (cf. Slater, *Dance of the Dolphin*), centers on the complete sexual seduction of a woman by the force of the sea as incarnate in the dolphin that lures her to her death in the waves. Although the dolphin is seen by most individuals as a "real" dolphin, he assumes for the objects of his seduction the figure of a beautiful naked man (not completely naked, since his genitals are covered). Throughout the film, it is the specter of his erotic nakedness that marks the temptations to which women are exposed as they sense him, see him, pursue him, and eventually embrace him and are drawn down to their watery death. The dolphin does assume other forms as well, and one important moment is when he appears as an American. His seductiveness in this sirenlike guise not only allows him access to the woman, but also to her husband, to whom he is alluring because of his promise of riches. This passing homoerotic note, however, is attenuated by the implication that the destructiveness of American values is just as seductive as the dolphin in his indigenous embodiment.

Clearly, Lima is working with an inversion of the legend of the siren who lures seafarers to death. In the case of the legend, men are the victims of an allegory of female hypersexual temptation, and as such it is clearly a replay of the seduction of Adam by Eve. In other versions of masculinity the man is supposed to be strong and wary enough to avoid the temptations of the woman and to resist them in those cases when she catches him off-guard: don't go near women, but if you can't avoid their company, be strong enough not to yield to their allure. In such a formulation, the unfortunate weakness of men is overshadowed by the unchecked sexuality of women, who are always ready to snare those who are careless. Moreover, such versions have no room for a distinction between female perfidy when it is a deliberate undertaking on the part of a woman and something that is beyond a woman's own control: woman as deliberately malicious Eve or woman as a victim of her uncontrollable drives. While it is generally assumed to be the latter, and women are damned accordingly, examples of the former circumstance hardly make matters any better.

An inversion of the significant roles of the legend of the siren leaves man as dangerous as woman as far as sexual appetite goes, and the siren is complemented by the legend of man as rapist. Women are cautioned to keep their distance from men and to protect themselves from their wiles, because all men want the same thing, and it is not the sanctity of womanhood (as the patriarchal vision would call it) or the integrity of women's bodies (as feminists would formulate it). Interestingly enough, in such interpretations of men's lives, the patriarchal code and some versions of feminism are in accord. The difference lies in the fact that the code of masculinity recognizes a *noblesse oblige* for a class of men: their sexual hygiene both strips them of bestial sensuality and conditions them to protect women from the depredations of common men as well as from themselves.

In Lima's film, the dolphin is, nevertheless, the embodiment of both wild male sexuality and female weakness, and the combination is a fatal one. Thus, toward the end of the film, the hunt for the dolphin by the village fishermen assumes virtually the dimensions of a Greek tragedy, as the grim-faced agents of the world as a male preserve undertake to destroy the mythic being that alternately challenges their sexual primacy (because he robs them of their women), imposes a norm of unfettered licentiousness (because he represents a sexual conduct that exists beyond the boundaries of a socially administered sexual economy), and models erotic exhibitionism (because the display of his body transgresses norms of concealment that can only be transgressed by tightly controlled forms of public sexual manifestations within the socially administered sexual economy).

Lima's film assumes a dimension beyond that of a sensationalist potboiler that allegorizes a tragico-pathetic story of the consequences of transgressing norms of sexual restraint and decency in the display of the male body. Film is notorious for its utilization of a display of the female body, as part of an ideology of female excess: it is as imperative to graphically define woman as a problem as to chart the consequences of what happens when woman as problem is allowed to slip out of control. Since it is unlikely to do more than allude obliquely to the naked female body before recent decades, filmmaking driven by such patriarchal versions of women's pathology insinuates the female body in metonymic and synecdochal fashions. After all, it would make little sense to claim that female sexuality is fatal to men and then to display unabashedly the body that is conventionally considered to be primarily the instrument of that sexuality (primarily, because, of course, there are at least psychological instruments as well that come into play). True, more recent filmmaking—and Brazil is no exception in following foreign examples and, indeed, in setting its own example— is almost totally explicit about the female body and female sexuality, subscribing to quite a different criterion whereby nudity only confirms the seductiveness of the female body, as though defying the spectator both to understand and to resist, despite whatever passing sexual arousal may take place. It is as though the medium of the film event ensured a distancing effect that prevents sexual arousal from having any real consequences.

One will note that "spectator" in the foregoing is unmarked for gender, since commercial mass-appeal films always assume that the viewer is male and that female viewers are going to view as males (feminist film criticism calls this "identifying with the oppressor") or at least that they are going to view as neutral social agents, distancing themselves from the specific female cases being portrayed on the screen. While women spectators may identify with female characters as victims and we must now understand that lesbian identification may also take place in ways that conventional film language can do nothing to control, conventional filmmaking as it continues to dominate the industry does nothing to create a specifically feminine/feminist point of view for the spectator, which is why so much women's and lesbians' filmmaking continues to be an alternative and dissenting cultural production. On a direct and superficial level, O boto does nothing to deviate from the representation of woman and female sexuality as problems and the inevitability (if not, as the film passingly suggests, the legitimacy) of male social agents' intervention in the woman's complete submission to the erotic fantasy the dolphin extends to her.

The film becomes problematical—and it is safe to assume that this is not a dimension sought by the director—in its display of the male body. Fleeting male nudity, especially when shot from the back, although occasionally frontal, has come to be expected in modern film, and there is no reason to believe that recent Brazilian productions would be any different. Such fleeting nudity serves only to give a more "contemporary" and audacious tinge to commercial productions. It may simply act as a sop to a presumed distaff demand that women have the same voyeuristic rights as men (one feminist counterargument is that female spectators are not interested in male nudity, which is simply one more objectification of the body, although there are advantages to be found in resisting such monolithic constructions of feminist mentality). Yet one can hardly contemplate the possibility that commercial filmmakers have any interest in catering to homoerotic interests in the male body, even if they might be pleased to capitalize on the sexual interest, no matter what quarter it might come from (straight, bisexual, or homoerotic), in circumstantial details of their productions.

However, what does in fact happen is that the human body of the dolphin, played by Carlos Alberto Ricelli (who will be seen two years later as the protagonist of *Jorge um brasileiro,* a movie in which his body is converted into an icon of Brazilian masculinity), while it still only appears fleetingly in the film, becomes a sign of wild male sexuality. The film prevents anyone other than selected women from seeing the dolphin's human body, which keeps Lima from having to address issues of pansexual if not directly homoerotic seduction and saves the male agents of social control from gazing/having to gaze on the nude male body (which is never shown frontally).

Yet, where the male agents of the film are "saved" from such an affront to manly decorum—healthy male sex drive, after all, cannot be confused with that of an erotic wild man—male spectators are not, opening up the possibility that O *boto* serves to promote scopic homoeroticism among all male viewers. If one could argue that Lima is asking the male spectator to identify with the wild sexuality of O *boto* to the extent that the film asks the audience to share in the pathos of both the woman's severance from decent society and the hunting down of the dolphin, it becomes impossible to know when the nude human presence of the dolphin is an embodiment of every man's will to be an object of lust and when it is an object of interested contemplation by every man, as much a subset of queer men as not. Videos—the major format in which film is now viewed in Latin America and almost everywhere else in the capitalist world—allow for slow motion, replay, and freeze frame, which are not available in movie-house viewing; this only means that the fleeting male nudity of *O boto*, no matter whom it is to be viewed by, with all sorts of attendant interpretations, can, by recourse to technical possibilities, be made much less fleeting.

I am not suggesting that *O boto* is a cryptogay film, as much as it is possible to view it in that fashion, with appropriate reassignment of roles whereby the female protagonist becomes a stand-in for the gay male in pursuit of the ideal masculine body. The tragico-pathetic ending of the film would thus be read as the violent reassertion of the heterosexist imperative in the face of homoerotic transgression, especially since the direct agent of the dolphin-man's death is his own son, anxious to avenge the affront deriving from the fact that the object of the father's attentions is the son's fiancee. The specter of incest only serves to further legitimate the reimposition of conventional sexuality, even if that sexuality is shown once again to be unstable when the son turns out to be interested in his mother. What I am suggesting is that the revision of the legend of the siren and the recourse to the recent possibilities in film of showing a measure of male nudity as a way of enhancing commercial interest contribute to a perturbation of the masculinist heterosexism, and therefore antifeminism, that otherwise dominates in the film.

Capitalismo selvagem

If Rui Guerra's 1986 *Ópera do malandro* thematizes capitalism of the Getúlio Vargas era and the transition from homely exploitation to the dynamics of international exchange, André Klotzel's 1993 *Capitalismo selvagem* models with exceptionally grotesque humor the working of killer capitalism as confirmed in Brazil by the implantation a year later of contemporary neoliberalism. José Mayer, one of Brazil's soap opera superstars, plays a tycoon, Hugo Assis, who leads a vast mining operation in Indian territory. The operation, Jota Mineração, which is interested in invading tribal lands for the purposes of extracting gold deposits, is itself a metaphor for economic development as a process of the rape and pillage of natural resources, and the film shows key images of the extensive high-tech operations that will virtually gobble up land and people in the maximization of its enterprise. Here too, as in *Ópera do malandro*, there is a feminine counterpart to the tycoon who in the end turns out to be the more effective leader. Indeed, in Klotzel's film, Diana, the wife of the tycoon, played by Marisa Orth, after having arranged her own "death" in order to engineer an anonymous vacation and pursue a sexual adventure, returns determined to take over the company from her husband, which she in fact is successful in doing. However, what Klotzel is doing is far from a sexist parody of the role female magnates and politicians have come to assume in contemporary Brazil. Rather, as will become clear in the comments below, he is detaching the masculinism of the magnate from a particular gender identity: if the female businesswoman in *Capitalismo selvagem* becomes more and more ruthless, in the accepted style of male corporate leaders, her discarded husband becomes feminized as he relinquishes corporate power. Thus, Klotzel is not telling us that women managers necessarily become like their male counterparts, only that some do, in their investment in a power struggle that is neither male nor female, but a reflex of power-driven masculinism.

Capitalismo selvagem adheres closely to the dramatic codes of Brazil's extremely successful and glossy television soap opera industry, which allows Klotzel's actors simply to recreate the sort of roles that they have come to be known for in that medium. Those codes involve stereotypic characters (the icy imperialism of the tycoon, the savage efficiency of his wife), plot developments that do not rely in any substantial way on narrative coherence (the fact that Assis turns out to be the survivor of an Indian tribe, esoteric pyrotechnics by the indigenous housekeeper who may in reality be his mother), the sudden importance of extraneous elements (the slapstick details of a journalist's relationship with her father and his death), the ostentatious display of sets that fulfill a fantasy of modernity (the palatial home of Assis-Medeiros, the vastness of the mining installations, the gloss and gleam of corporate headquarters), and the recourse to *deus ex machina* occurrences that are not justified by the narrative logic (Diana's sudden return from the grave). It is not that such elements are not narratively possible, but rather that, in the framework of the soap opera, the need to make them plausible in terms of narrative expectations or horizons of narrative knowledge is not of primary concern. Rather, what is of primary concern is keeping the story moving along at a fast pace so that a particular rhythm of exposition is maintained, with this rhythm being of greater importance than narrative logic.

From another point of view, *Capitalismo selvagem* is a parody of soap opera productions. This is particularly evident in the way in which the actors seem to be winking at the public as they enact their corresponding roles, particularly Marisa Orth, whose seduction of one of her male employees confirms her status as a take-charge woman. Once she has removed her own panties, she hangs them on the doorknob of the office as a sort of Do Not Disturb sign before proceeding with the business at hand. José Mayer's lapses into epilepsy—an objective correlative in the film of his Indian roots and the devastation of having abandoned them—and the tipsiness of the journalist, Elisa Medeiros (Fernanda Torres), who goes to interview him and finds herself the guest of honor in an intimate tête-à-tête are hilarious moments in the film, as are the two major scenes of lovemaking, one in a lush city park and the other in the return to innocence Elisa engineers for the two of them.

However, what most confirms the parodic dimension of *Capitalismo selvagem* is the sense of what meaningful narrative construction is involved—in fact, one could argue that the presence of narrative construction, rather than merely a disjointed series of scenes constructed on the basis of soap opera clichés, is the central parody of Klotzel's film. Elisa, who falls in love with Hugo, a love that is confirmed by her discovery that he is in fact of indigenous descent, is determined to lead him back to a condition of human decency, which is manifested first by his abandoning his chauffeured limousine and leading her into the thick forest of the park for lovemaking au naturel and then by his abandon to the lure of nature as the two of them disappear beneath the animistic waters of the jungle, lost forever to the corrupting civilization symbolized by Jota Mineração. In the final frame of the film, we see what remains of their clothing floating on the surface of the water. Elisa, as a feminine force of nature, has consumed Hugo in what is undoubtedly a parody of numerous pretexts, especially Joaquim Pedro de Andrade's *Macunaíma* (1969), itself based on an important Modernist parody, Mário de Andrade's novel by the same name from 1928. It may be questionable whether or not this represents any sort of salvation for Hugo from destructive macho forces. But what is particularly funny for the sense of the film is that Hugo ends up as much controlled by Elisa as he was by Diana, and one can hardly miss the vaginal dimension of the maelstrom that swallows him up.

Klotzel's film is a denial of triumph in modern business as a legitimate personal and social goal. Many soap operas in fact concern themselves with the underbelly of the institutions of power and influence of modernity, particularly the board room, such as Rede Globo's highly successful *O dono do mundo* (The Owner of the World, early 1990s). Such products in fact relegitimize what they may criticize: the excesses of individuals are questioned, but not the legitimacy of the institution, and the reigning ideology is that such institutions, which have a rightful place in the natural order, will function for the social good if it is possible to get rid of the individuals whose ambition undermines their efficaciousness.

By contrast, *Capitalismo selvagem* portrays the institution of Jota Mineração as evil, something that is not difficult to do, given its commercial activity, and the human agents are only an extension of its essential meaning. Thus, Hugo and Elisa's flight is a repudiation of the whole complex of modernity as symbolized by the firm, while perhaps at the same time parodying, in a second instance, the idea of the possibility of flight from modern society, of a return to an uncontaminated nature and to a lost innocence. Such a possibility is also parodied, it would seem, by the clichés surrounding the couple's sinking into the bosom of the water spirit Z: the new age music, the pantomime of allurement and engulfment, and the transparent detail of the city clothes that float to the surface.

But there is another significant way in which *Capitalismo selvagem* breaks with the dominant schemes that are recycled by the soap opera, in which strong female figures only mean the intervention of phallic women and virtually no questioning of the institution of the patriarchy that sustains capitalism and masculinist

*Video promotion for **Capitalismo selvagem**.*
Reproduced by permission of Sagres Home Video Ltd.

society. In Klotzel's film, despite the presence of José Mayer, whom the spectator is accustomed to seeing in strong central roles (e.g., the highly successful miniseries based on Rubem Fonseca's 1990 novel *Agosto*, in which the personal drama of a Raymond Chandler–like police agent played by Mayer is juxtaposed to the events surrounding the suicide of the strongman president Getúlio Vargas in August 1954), three influential women impinge on Hugo's life in ways that lead up to his flight from civilization.

In terms of the narrative exposition of the film, the first of these three women is the newspaper reporter, Elisa, who goes to interview him about the reports that Jota Mineração is to invade Indian lands in order to extract gold deposits. Elisa is unprepared for the seduction scenario Hugo has organized for her, but, in the best clichéd fashion of the soap operas *Capitalismo* is parodying, her innocence prevails: it is she who seduces him, leading him away from the life of exploitation, the savage capitalism, in which he is a feared tycoon to return to the "savagery" of untainted nature. Now, Brazilian soap operas are not likely to promote either saving innocence or the allure of an untainted nature. Parody enters in the assumption that role reversal, that major shifts in human motivation, can readily be affected by a commanding human presence, whether that presence is a dominant sexual figure (the principal plot-motivating device of the bulk of soap operas, whether a seductive woman or an overpowering man) or, in this case, a sweet flower of innocence. The very fact that this sort of figure can steer a powerful magnate away from his heady life of economic and political power is an outrageous proposition, and in the soap-opera world Klotzel recreates in his film it is so over the top of genre conventions that it functions to parody that narrative world.

The second female figure to exercise an influence over Hugo is his wife, Diana, presumed dead in an airplane crash. When she unexpectedly reappears—and in this Klotzel does make "straight" use of a stock soap-opera device: the unexpected plot reversal based on the demonstration that something is not as it had appeared to be (in this case, that Diana was not really dead)—Hugo's empire is thrown into turmoil because she is determined to wrest final control away from her ineffectual husband. With key positions in the hands of family and lovers, Diana wishes to proceed unchecked with the mining operations, and not even the invasion of corporate headquarters by members of the irate Indian tribe whose lands will be destroyed by the operation can deter her. Elisa, in her desire to defend the Indians' rights and to win Hugo, is placed in a confrontational position with Hugo's wife in a contest between Good and Evil as allegorized in competing female characters. Elisa cannot stop Jota Mineração's operations—and Klotzel in this accurately models the unchecked invasion of tribal lands that characterizes the multinational and neoliberal capitalism that currently holds sway in Brazil—but she can at least wrest Hugo from the world that has corrupted his soul of a Noble Savage. The fits of epilepsy Hugo experiences (which may or may not be induced by his mother) are undoubtedly a reflex of the struggle of his indigenous roots, which in his rise to power he has denied, to reassert themselves. There is a marvelously extravagant scene in the movie when Elisa goes to see Hugo at corporate headquarters. Suddenly the entire office is invaded by the lush jungle, complete with the call of wild birds and the buzz of insects. As an objective correlative of his noble past that Elisa wishes to restore to him, Hugo's epilepsy can only be read by his wife as a sign of her husband's fatal weakness as a corporate leader.

Finally, there is the creepy presence of the domestic employee who turns out to be Hugo's indigenous mother. Totally out of place in the high-tech gloss of the Assis's absolutely top-of-the-line residence, this woman appears and disappears unexpectedly like a malevolent gnome. But she and Elisa will become allies in the project to save her son from the full force of modern corporate life as represented by the savage business world. Hugo's mother's influence seems to work in the following fashion: while he and Diana are confronting representatives of the indigenous tribes in corporate headquarters, Hugo is struck on the head by one of his wife's thugs so that it will look like he is the victim of violence at the hands of the indigenous protestors; Hugo goes into an epileptic fit. We see his mother, meanwhile, having similar convulsions (death throes?). Some mysterious process of identification with her son's seizure is the cause of her convulsions. As he writhes in agony, we see her in a hospital bed, connected to the usual high-tech monitoring devices, the symbols of the imprisonment by modernity to which both she and her son are victim, as well as their fellow tribe members. The action slices back to Hugo, who has been stretched out on a desk top; as he comes to, he begins to speak in the indigenous language of the tribal representatives: apparently his mother has exercised a telepathic influence that has allowed him to recover his native language.

The film ends with Diana and one of her henchmen celebrating their triumph in a tropical vacation setting, while Hugo and Elisa have returned with the tribal representatives to their ancestral village. In the final sequence, they sink beneath the waters of a lagoon. This rather narratively jumbled conclusion, intercut with scenes from the four narrative threads—the invasion of corporate headquarters, the escape by Diana and brother/lover?/henchman, Hugo's mother in intensive care, and Hugo and Elisa's "return to paradise"—underscores how tenuous cause and effect can be in the sort of television narrative *Capitalismo* is parodying.

Klotzel's film is of interest for a redefinition of masculine roles in its depiction of Hugo's domination by women. There is an inversion of the image of the unfettered captain of industry, the corporate tycoon responsible in his power to no one: such a role serves to affirm an ideal paradigm of masculinism. Nevertheless, the Hugo that emerges from behind the mask of cool self-control that we see him wearing in the first scenes in the film when he receives Elisa in his posh living room has little to do with the model of masculine autonomy. Dominated by Diana and watched over by his mother, Hugo succumbs to the allure of Elisa's innocence, thereby paving the way for his mother to exercise her defining control in bringing about his reintegration with his native roots. The fact that in Klotzel's movie this turn of events is meant to constitute a redemption for Hugo (whose last name evokes the worldly renunciations of St. Francis) does not change the fact that it is predicated on a crisis of masculinity in terms of the power hegemony, which depends on the sort of controlled self-containment Hugo can no longer exercise, although his wife seems to be quite comfortable and competent in filling the vacuum left by his disappearance.

It is noteworthy that *Capitalismo selvagem* makes no gesture toward social redemption, and in this it is also adhering, if parodically, to the ideological principles of the soap opera: the world is about individuals and never about collective social experience. Moreover, individual histories can never be allegories of the social—as is the case, for example, with *Jorge um brasileiro, A hora da estrela*, or *O beijo no asfalto*. Thus, the return to paradise also figures as an escape from an immutable social reality, which is what we understand from the triumphalism of Diana and her lover in their own tropical paradise, the vacation retreat for the wealthy they escape to rather than continue to tolerate the useless confrontation staged by the invading tribal representatives. *Capitalismo selvagem* may indicate something of a social shift: after all, in democratic Brazil, the indigenous people can demand their rights, and women can move into positions of power and influence. In the former case, the Indians constitute no real threat to the economic and political system, and Jota Mineração is able to proceed unhindered in its mineral exploitation of tribal lands. And in the second case, Diana is nothing but the epitomization of the phallic woman. Indeed, her exercise of masculine power is ultimately more effective than that of her ineffectual husband, weakened by the combined effects of epilepsy and love. His renewed ability to speak his native indigenous language is but the definitive marker of his alienation from the power he once held: alongside the status of Portuguese as the language of masculine power, the indigenous languages are the markers of feminization, since in their fragmentation and their isolation within the overarching modern state they are unable to compete with the language of economic and political hegemony.

Capitalismo selvagem aspires to little more than a genial parody of soap opera narratives, but in the process it also, like *Ópera do malandro,* sketches the outlines of the new capitalism being practiced in Brazil in the past decade. In the fashion of the rhetorical figure of the zeugma, it plays on the use of the word *selvagem* both to describe a particular brand of cutthroat business practices and at the same time to allude to a return to the "savage" qualities of precapitalist society—signaled, certainly with grim irony, by the mythological dimensions of Diana's name. The film is not ingenious enough to constitute a Brazilian equivalent of Pedro Almodóvar's deconstructive interpretations of Spanish modernity, but it is effective in its very funny critical modeling of the dynamics of Brazilian capitalism. And since capitalism is unquestionably the economic model that accompanies and sustains the masculinist patriarchy, by putting into question Hugo's participation in the former, Klotzel's film essentially rewrites the conditions, through the triumph of a feminist principle, of his participation in the latter. This rewriting is basically incoherent and preposterous and in no way consonant with any model of theoretical feminism in the service of social reconstruction. Yet it is just scandalous enough to provide a quirky edge to Klotzel's film that makes it of interest as an interpretation of gender roles in contemporary Brazil.

Yndio do Brasil

Sylvio Back has created for himself a distinguished career as Brazil's first truly postmodern film director (see *Sylvio Back: Filmes noutra margem*). He has more than thirty films to his credit, with an emphasis on deconstructive documentaries. While it has become urgent to deconstruct the documentary, especially as it relates to subaltern social subjects (the documentary committed to "giving voice" to marginal groups), this has usually meant a number of limited options: (1) docudrama, in which fictional enactments complement archival material (cf. *Que bom te ver viva*, discussed elsewhere in this study, and my essay on Raúl A. Tosso's *Gerónima* [Argentina, 1985]: Foster, *Contemporary Argentine Cinema* 66–79); (2) complete fictional enactment of a sociologically verifiable theme, as in Héctor Babenco's *At Play in the Fields of the Lord* (1991), in which a Brazilian indigenous culture is fabricated, including, with the assistance of anthropological linguistics, a language for it; (3) a distancing from the material being presented by refusing to engage in the voice-over narrative that provides an interpretive—and, therefore, biased (usually in terms of so-called liberal values)—commentary, a sort of conceptual guide for what is being presented. None of these options resolves the problem of inserting a controlling perspective into the document, but they do serve to disrupt, or at least undertake to disrupt, the seamless fabric of a conceptually coherent interpretation that drives the high-minded documentary, especially those (as in the title of Burton's collection of essays, *The Social Documentary*) documentaries made for social change.

Back breaks significantly with many of the prevailing conventions of the documentary, and the postmodern attitude of his work implies the futility of the attempt to distinguish between the documentary and fiction, on the one hand, and, on the other, the imperative to question at what point in the social text it is clear that a parodic, ironic, and deconstructive voice can effectively be inserted. Known for the work he has done on (the numbers he has done on, one might say) paradigmatic Brazilian sociohistoric myths, such as on Germans in Brazil (*Aleluia, Gretchen* [1976]) or on the much vaunted Brazilian expeditionary force in World War II (*Rádio Auriverde* [1987]), Back is as much interested in critiquing the sociohistoric myths as he is in analyzing the genres of cultural production available for recounting those myths.

Yndio do Brasil (1995) is one of Back's most recent and most elaborate reworkings of the documentary genre.[4] At first appearance, one might almost assume that the text is a hoax, in the sense that there appears to be no clear structure of development, no overarching point is being directly articulated through a sustained voice-over commentary, and no attempt is made to analyze the archival footage that extends over approximately a fifty-year period, as though the requirement to assess sources were impertinent. Moreover, it is not always clear what sources are fictional (e.g., films in which the Indian is thematized or indigenous culture is part of the backdrop for yet one more exotic jungle picture) and what sources are documentary, particularly in the forms of newsreels and government propaganda clips (often both categories yield the same texts).

For example, the playbill for *Yndio do Brasil* is headed by the statement "O único índio bom é o índio filmado" (The only good Indian is a filmed Indian), a clear reference to the infamous phrase, attributed to Philip Henry Sheridan, that "the only good Indian is a dead Indian." The image accompanying this text consists of an Indian, in black and white but with a colored feather, adopting a "what's this?" pose, arms extended in defense, legs apparently ready to jump back if need be, confronting an image on the left (the privileged position in a culture that reads from left to right) of a professional moving-picture camera with its lens extended in a direct line to the Indian's head, as though "shooting" the Indian, but with the legs of its tripod also bent in order to facilitate either an aggressive advance or a hasty retreat—although, since what is offered is a record of the filming of the Indian, it certainly must be preferentially the former option. This image stresses the materiality of the filming of the Indian and the materiality of the cultural exchange that is effected through the imposition on the Indians of the "gifts" that the Europeans bestow on them. The film record of such an imposition is equally the assimilation of the Indian to European culture through an instrument, the camera, of that culture's cultural production, and in this sense it also contributes to the Indian's "reduction" to European society. Hence the validity of the image of the camera as an extension of the aggression against the Indian of European culture.

Back reveals an unquestioned commitment to analyzing in a critical fashion how the Indian has been filmed in Brazilian culture (another whole chapter is how indigenous culture has been transcribed in American filmmaking) and how that filming has contributed to the extermination of the Indian in a society in which there are now more native speakers of Japanese than there are of all the indigenous languages put together (David Viñas has written that the Indians of Argentina were its first "disappeared persons" [*Indios, ejército y frontera,* 12]). Filmmaking has contributed to extermination by circulating stereotypes of the indigenous population that have contributed to neglect, hostility, patronizing attitudes, and inscription in Western ways that the infrastructure and local economy of indigenous peoples cannot sustain. As one government clip asserts, supported by the usual image of the smiling chieftain, the group in question took immediately to Western ways without any resistance.

Significantly, there is no dialogue in any of this material in which the indigenous peoples speak, whether in their own tribal languages or in Portuguese. Of course, Back's film complements the enormous efforts that have been made in Brazil by indigenous people since the return to institutional democracy in 1985 to establish bases of political power and to engage in a proactive role with state agencies concerned with the affairs of native peoples. *Yndio do Brasil* is only one of a number of cultural products that attest to efforts being made to provide a representation of indigenous culture that can attempt to evade the now centuries-old structures of oppression and extermination, such as the project in São Paulo of the internationally known Brazilian anthropologist Darcy Ribeiro (the Fundação Memorial da América Latina) or the 1985 television program by O Globo on the Alto Xingu (the Xingu is one of the major tributaries of the Amazon to the south and a spinal column for an extensive concentration of indigenous cultures in the country).

Back uses the film and TV star José Mayer to dramatize cultural material relating to the Indian that non-natives have written, in the fashion of texts that attempt honestly, if not always successfully, to speak for those who have no voice of their own—i.e., who have no way of connecting with the discourse structures of the dominant society, since it is not always a question of language but of knowing how communication is organized. Early in the film, the following text is incorporated:

Índio da América,
fizemos nosso catecismo
para seu suicídio amargo
fizemos nosso catecismo
para seu suicídio caro.[5]

And toward the end, after viewing a litany of images that confirm the construction of an exterminating catechism by European society, Mayer affirms that indigenous culture has become:

um pai sem país
um país sem pãi.[6]

This couplet plays on the similarity of the word for country (*país*) and the plural (*pães*) of the word for father (these poetic texts by Back, written for the film, are published in Back, *Yndio do Brasil: Poemas do filme*). While reinvesting in the patriarchal notion of the defining stature of the father figure, the point of the couplet is the destruction of a social system: without the semiotic center of the father, society collapses, and what tenuous social organization is left has no semiotic center.

In this sense, *Yndio do Brasil* approaches the issue of the crisis of masculinity from a different point of view than the films dealing with contemporary urban society. Clearly, it cannot be a question of contemporary urban society reduplicating its own crises of masculinity in the organization of indigenous society, since, precisely, the process of extermination, the suicide that is both bitter and costly, was put in place during moments of social history in which a dominant masculinism was what allowed no room for the survival of the indigenous people. That is, the masculinism of the former necessitated the destruction of the fathers of the latter.

It is interesting to note that the clips Back has chained together focus primarily on masculine bodies, perhaps in part to eschew the voyeurism of female nudity that has always been privileged in commercial films in which the body of woman, always seen as the axis of the problems that drive the narrative plot, is privileged. These masculine bodies are presented—that is, the clips are chosen so that these bodies are presented—essentially in positions of nudity, and not always protected by a loincloth. Such a representation underscores the radical Otherness of the native Indians, something which, despite the protestations to the effect that they have willingly and, indeed, joyfully accepted the beneficent civilizing effect of Western ways, can never be overlooked in the actual material filmic representations they are given. Conjoined over and over again with representatives of the socially dominant sectors—why else would they be shown, since their only importance must lie in their interaction with those dominant sectors?—they are marked as radically different not only by the fact that they do not speak and that the elements of their culture that are recorded are exclusively those that relate to the concerns of the voices of power, but also by the fact that they are physically cast in terms of difference.

Moreover, this difference results in a desexualization that infantilizes them. I do not know if Back has deliberately chosen clips in which indigenous buttocks are prominently displayed, but such a display can only be acceptable (that is, any display that would be unacceptable for whatever reason would simply be edited out of a film, if filmed in the first place) if it is vacant of sexual meaning or if any sexual meaning there from another social symbolic perspective is drained from it completely. The wholesale draining of sexual meaning from collective social subjects (i.e., not from a specific subject, whose sexuality may be canceled out for symbolically greater reasons—e.g., the pope) such as a tribe of Indians can only serve to infantilize them because it forces them back into a period of imagined innocence in which their bodies are denied sexual meaning (or any sexual meaning attached to them can only be perverse). Male nudity, even if "only" the display of the buttocks, is a firm taboo in Western filmmaking, and Brazilian production is no exception; indeed, it still often seems, with all of the breaching of taboos, that mature male genitalia are more easily displayed than buttocks. And this is perhaps also the case because folk wisdom assigns to the buttocks the locus of homoerotic, and therefore transgressive nonheterosexual, desire. That is, the buttocks are the locus in such a figuring of the demasculinization and hence, in an inevitable gender binary, the feminization of an individual. Moreover, it is a depiction of the body as especially vulnerable to sudden physical attack.

Yndio begins with a camera shot of a fallen Indian, focusing in slow motion on his naked body in general and his buttocks in particular. This long shot foreshadows the reinscription of the Indian and the body of the Indian in Back's documentary. Since the documentary will resemanticize the filming of the Indian, deconstructing the way in which the Indian is feminized by European society and possessed, assimilated by the camera, a prefigurative shot like this suggests the return of the Indian body to a prefeminized state, to the fully meaningful masculinity of a historical and therefore sexualized body. Yet, ironically, since the body's nakedness is still being interpreted by the modes of cultural production of the camera, its resexualization now borders on the homoerotic via the male director's contemplation of its newly significant sexuality—or soon to be newly significant as the documentary proceeds to deconstruct the strategies of feminization and desexualization.

There can be little question that, except for the way in which such an anatomical display may be of interest to some gay viewers, the display of male buttocks in *Yndio do Brasil* is of no sexual interest because it is an aspect of the nonthreatening status recognized for the Indian. Certainly, the Indian is nonthreatening because desexualized, to the degree that sexual threat (cf. images of the black rapist in U.S. society evoked in so many films) is the paradigm of social threat. That the indigenous peoples are no longer any threat because those that have not been exterminated have been civilized and that their bodies have no sexual meaning are two propositions that are correlated in the clips assembled by Back: under the umbrella of the ideology of One Brazil that one propaganda clip promotes, the Indian is a happy child. Of course, other social subjects are equally infantilized by such an ideology, but some of the grinning children in the propaganda clip will grow up to be the agents of the state who control the lives of the perpetual child the Indian has become.

Back titles his film with an archaic form of the Portuguese word for Indian, and one suspects that this is to capture how the documentary record of destruction reaches far enough back to reveal such archaic uses. The filmed record is not yet one hundred years old, barely one-fifth the age of the written record, dating back to the early sixteenth century. But the ideology of the film record is unquestionably of a whole with the first written sources, and there is no question that the other semiotic systems present in *Yndio do Brasil*—for example, the European music of epic and triumphal connotation and the recurring language of civilizing domination and its attendant discourses—serve to reinforce the filmic language in which the powerful images of trivialization confirm how the Brazilian Indian has been demasculinized and disempowered long before anyone got around to filming him (Back's archival sources) or refilming him (Back's text).

Finally, it is instructive to view Back's film in the context of one of the urtexts of Brazilian culture, José de Alencar's Romantic *O guarani* (The Guarani Indian, 1857), in which the Indian dies at the end of the novel by being swept away in an apocalyptic flood, symbolizing the washing clean of the slate of the Brazilian landscape for the European inhabitant. Carlos Gomes produced an opera based on the novel in the early part of this century, and it was recorded on film in 1916 (there is no known director in the contemporary cinematographic sense of the word). Back's film thus functions also as a critical rereading of this foundational Romantic fantasy of the necessary disappearance of the Indian from the Brazilian landscape.

The six films that have been dealt with in this section all directly or implicitly involve a questioning of masculine subjectivity. While only a film like *Yndio do Brasil* really comes close to questioning conventional constructions of masculinity, all can be read in ways to bring up such issues. While contestatory readings forefronted in cultural products are always to be prized, my interest with the majority of these films is in the way in which features of the text may be said to provoke in viewers a contestatorial reading at their interpretive level. Thus, I have noted the particular rhetorical highlighting of a hypermasculinity in the case of *Jorge um brasileiro* and *Lamarca*. The two films look toward different political periods, the first toward postdictatorship and the second to the armed struggle against the dictatorship. But both highlight echoes of the Brazilian mythical superman and, because they are films, both make use of a hypermasculinity that enables one to raise questions about the latent eroticism of a highly charged homosocialism that is the base of the group solidarity being modeled.

In the case of *Ópera do malandro* and *Capitalismo selvagem,* masculinity is connected to issues of economic development. Whether or not one subscribes to specific Marxian views, the economy is, really, the driving force of Brazilian society—or so one would deduce from its centrality in these two films. The interplay of masculine types, and of feminine counterparts, in *Ópera* is directly related to an interpretation of Brazil's transition from a precapitalist feudalism to U.S.-dominated capitalism and, projectively, to neoliberal globalization. In the case of *Capitalismo,* as a feature of neoliberal globalization, a barracuda-like businesswoman outmachos the macho captain of industry, whose feminization in the film is as much a utopian opting out of late capitalism—a capitalism it appears to be too late for Brazil to opt out of—as it is the radical, inevitable marking of the man who can no longer relate to its severe demands.

Finally, *O boto,* like *Yndio do Brasil,* stands somewhat outside of the central core of these films, which deal predominantly with late-twentieth-century urban life in Brazil. If one deals in a contestatorial way with the historical treatment of the Indian, the other uses conventional rural mythology, as I have argued, to show that prevailing sexual categories are a part of modern social definitions. Moreover, one of the interests of rural mythological tropes, in addition to other "transgressions" such as that between humans and animals, may also involve alternate views of masculine categories of interest and be available to popular culture reformulation precisely because they demonstrate still valid, if only residual, gender troubles.

CHAPTER 2

Constructions of Feminine and Feminist Identities

"Que bom te ver viva" *(How nice to see you alive)*
— EPONYMIC EXPRESSION FROM A
BRAZILIAN DOCUMENTARY

One of the social consequences of the return to institutional democracy in the 1980s in the wake of the neofascist dictatorships in Latin America was the ability to pursue a cultural production that showed how social subjects who had formerly been at the mercy of tyranny now had the potential, no matter how minimal, of becoming agents of their own destiny or at least of achieving a level of consciousness with regard to this potential. The creation of images of such agency necessarily affects the population as a whole, since one of the distinguishing characteristics is the virtually complete suppression of social agency under the sign of military tyranny: even those who believe that by supporting the dictatorship they are protected, and thus have some measure of agency, may find that this agency will disappear on a whim (cf. the situation of the main protagonist in the Argentine Luis Puenzo's 1985 *La historia oficial* [The Official Story]: Foster, *Contemporary Argentine Cinema*, 38–54).

But if cultural production models (the promise of) agency for the citizenry at large, there are subsets that focus primarily on a specific subaltern group or on an intersection of groups. On the one hand, the question of agency may be implicit in works that concern themselves primarily with the reasons for social marginalization and the conditions of subalternity. These are works that analyze the social text, with or without a historical dimension, in order to underscore the ways in which social groups are marginal and how that marginality may have been particularly effected by the dictatorship or how the latter clarified a structure of marginalization that is inherent in the sociopolitical history of the country, only to be magnified by tyranny. The films of Héctor Babenco, an Argentine who came to work in Brazil at the time of the military coup in his country in 1976, exemplify this possibility: children in *Pixote* (1981), social underdogs in *Lúcio Flávio, o passageiro da agonia* (Lúcio Flávio, the Passenger of Agony, 1977), and a lost Indian tribe in *At Play in the Fields of the Lord* (1991).

Carlos Diegues's *Xica da Silva* (1976) clearly exemplifies the possibility of creating a happy ending through the restoration of social agency. Indeed, Diegues's film version of the life of Silva, an eighteenth-century black slave who attained social power and position through the manipulation of a white lover, a crown representative, corrects the ending of Antonio Callado's play *O tesouro de Chica da Silva* (The Treasure of Chica da Silva), in his *A revolta da cachaça: Teatro negro* (The Rum Revolt: Black Theater, 1983; originally staged in 1958). In Callado's play, Silva necessarily falls from grace when her lover is called back to Portugal: it is simply too much of a contradiction of social history for a black slave woman to exercise power, and the violation to the social code of such an aberrant fact is the sense of the play. In Diegues's film, although Silva also necessarily gets her comeuppance, in the spirit of the need to foreshadow the redemocratization of Brazil, there is kind of a rollicking Disney ending in which a flight of fancy suspends the rigors of the social text (which earlier has involved explicit scenes of the torture of prisoners) to suggest that Xica's sexuality and *joie de vivre* will see her through a temporary setback. However, the need to project some sense of optimism in a movie that, during the dictatorship, represents the institutions of slavery and torture as figures of life under the military carries the day in Diegues's film, as part of a transcendence of the confines of exclusive social denunciation (see Araujo, "The Spheres of Power").

Of specific interest to this chapter are issues relating to women's history in contemporary Brazil, where in a documentary mode, as with *Que bom te ver viva*—in which the question of women's marginalization crosses with the specific facts of arrest, torture, and incarceration of women for political activities—or in a complex fictional elaboration like *A hora da estrela*—in which there is a crushing accumulation of evidence of women's disappearance as social subjects (by contrast to their overwhelming visibility as masculinist stereotypes) that becomes figured in the film as a fatal accident at the hands of the instruments of patriarchal repression. *Eternamente Pagu* is, by contrast to these two extremes, an example of documentary fiction, in the sense that it is based on the historical record but utilizes fictional narration in order to construct a coherent interpretation of the problematics of a woman's presence in the foreground of the stage of important national political events. The impossibility of such a project is depicted in terms of the violent circumscription of social subjectivity Pagu thinks in the beginning she may have (as contrasted to the zero-level of self-awareness shown by Macabea, the "heroine" of *A hora da estrela*).

Such a circumscription is even more vividly evident in *Bananas Is My Business*, also a very successful intersection of documentary and fictional narration, because it focuses on the famous movie star and singer Carmen Miranda, for many an icon of Brazilian national identity and female sexuality. With the exception of the pronouncedly pathetic "absent" social subjectivity of Macabea, these films have in common the ways in which the presumed strength of character of archetypes of contemporary Brazilian women—professionals, film stars, political activists—is illusory, to the extent that any real exercise of social subjectivity results in forms of direct aggression (persecution, imprisonment, torture, death) or indirect application of punitive, but no less effectively violent, consequences (family problems, substance abuse, alienation, frustration, futile emotional reactions).

A hora da estrela

Suzana Amaral's *A hora da estrela* (1985), loosely based on the 1977 novel of the same name by Clarice Lispector (who died of cancer the year it was published), is quite another matter. The film centers on Macabea (brilliantly played by Marcélia Cartaxo), a young woman from the Brazilian Nordeste who has ended up in São Paulo. She is typical of the tide of migrants in Brazil, who, echoing similar internal movements in other Latin American countries, flood into major metropolitan areas seeking employment. Usually willing to work for the most minimal wages and to occupy crowded and substandard rooming houses (which often means sharing a communal bedroom with strangers and lining up for scarce bathroom facilities), these individuals are virtual zombies in the urban landscape. While some may turn to crime or find other less precarious means of livelihood, the majority of them wander the city seeking an escape from the tedium of their existence, from the ugliness of the workplace and the discomfort of their rooms, but they are too poorly paid to avail themselves of anything more than the most primitive amenities of the city. Many of them send money home, and many of them lose what scant wages they earn to big-city hustlers and thieves. Women are perennially vulnerable to exploitation; a seduction may leave them as unmarried mothers and/or prostitutes.

Large urban centers have always attracted the miscellaneous elements of modern society. But Latin American countries like Brazil, with a vast outback offering few opportunities for survival, not to mention the Nordeste wasteland, where droughts make rural life even more precarious than usual, can do little to impede the steady influx of the impoverished into metropolitan areas. Moreover, the urban economy requires such an influx, because without cheap labor for whom the worst workplace and living conditions are better than anything at home, much of the life of the big city would come to a standstill. Individuals like Macabea are the modern-day slaves who keep the economy going, and they stand at the base of the extensive human infrastructure that ensures the stability of the privileged. Amaral's film ends with Macabea being run down in the street by a sleek, sexual-fantasy beautiful man of the privileged class. The symbolism is painfully obvious: Macabea is a disposable drone in a vast economic network whose surplus value produces the sleekness and the other trappings of material well-being as evidenced by the man who slams into her.

The organizing principle of Amaral's film is Macabea's profound ugliness, bordering on the grotesque. She is not monstrous in any way, but as far as the conventions of feminine attractiveness in Brazil are concerned she is completely and utterly graceless: her features are the quintessence of plainness, her clothes are the nadir of style, and her physical mannerisms—the most graphic one is wiping her perpetually runny nose on her clothes—are the ground zero of slovenliness. She rarely has anything to say, and that rarely in a complete sentence; moreover, when she speaks, she does so in an accent that is socially unacceptable in a society in which language plays an immensely important discriminating role. Her work skills are almost ludicrous; and her general stance toward life is that of a startled deer. She negotiates relations with others by the monotonous and insistent repetition of the apologetic "Desculpe" (Excuse me), and it is as if she has no memory reserves whatever to draw upon to provide her with experiences of pleasure and fulfillment.

In this sense, Macabea is a dense icon of the social circumstances of the rural immigrant lost in the big city as much as she synthesizes the image that self-styled sophisticated city dwellers have of the hoards of rural people who crowd the city: the latter, with their modest clothes, clumsy ways, and laughable accents, are convenient scapegoats, but rarely are they recognized for their contribution to the amenities enjoyed by the former. Caught between these two symbolic positions, Macabea's role in the film is to enact over and over again, in scene after scene, the conditions of her marginalization. Amaral has chosen with extreme care an inventory of metonymic situations for Macabea to demonstrate her marginalization: her repeated humiliations because of her clerical ineptitude, her personal hygiene, her social gaucheries, her inability to relate to other people, and on and on in an oppressively dismal accumulation. It is a demonstration that she makes to those around her (including even her fellow immigrants), to the spectators of the film (who presumably belong essentially to the social classes who live on the shoulders of the Macabeas), and, most importantly, to herself. Macabea's sense of abjection is overwhelming, and she is a walking self-fulfilling prophecy of gloom and doom.

Amaral has, in a word, created the antitype of the stereotypical woman—and just to make sure the spectator cannot miss the point, such a woman is coded into the film as Macabea's colleague. Glória is a paradigmatic self-indulgent, carefree survivor of the urban rat race and the war of the sexes. She knows exactly how to land on her feet no matter what situation comes along, and she is proud of her ability to handle men, to juggle several relationships at the same time, and to derive the maximum profit in exchange for her favors. Her lying and scheming are hardly manifestations of a cynicism she has chosen as a way of life. Rather, they are her well-honed tools for survival in a very hostile world, and she is so transparent in her utilization of skills that the spectator, more occupied with cringing in the face of Macabea's abjection, has little time to condemn her. Glória typifies the way things are, especially for a single woman, and there is not much more to be said.

Macabea meets a two-bit Romeo in the park one weekend. Olímpico turns out also to be from the Nordeste, and the two see each other casually and painfully without really being lovers, although it is clear that Olímpico is on the make for something better than Macabea's very low-calorie companionship. When Glória decides to hustle Olímpico, it is not so much a low-down betrayal of Macabea (whom she genuinely befriends on several occasions) as it is an aesthetic exercise: Olímpico comes into view as another male body to be used and discarded, and Glória sets to work to see what there is in it for her. When she sees it's not likely to be much, she kicks him aside as casually as he had Macabea: the cruelest scene in a movie filled with the heedless cruelty of hardscrabble urban existence is when Olímpico tells Macabea to get lost: she is nothing more than a hair in his soup.

Amaral made her film around the same time that the rising international star Sônia Braga was making some of her well-known soft porn movies. *A dama do lotação* (The Lady on the Bus), on the sexual frustrations of a lonely housewife who rides the bus in search of the press of human contact, is from 1978, while *Eu te amo* (I Love You), on the sexual high jinks of bored pseudointellectuals, is from 1980. Braga is an icon of the sensuous, sexy Brazilian woman who is the mainstay of tourist posters, the woman who may be intelligent, accomplished, successful, but who has not "lost" her femininity and the awareness of her own body and the talent to use it as an erotic display text. Such a woman may not always move skillfully through the world, but the reigning proposition is that she is as much respected for her sense of womanhood as she is exploited for it, providing a tension that makes such women, like Xica da Silva, tremendously important cultural semiotic signs in the cultural interpretation of the Brazilian social text. In *A hora da estrela,* Glória may be almost a parody of this sort of typical Brazilian hot-shot woman. Films made at the same time with actresses like Sônia Braga provide an important intertext, and any of these women are monuments to an institution of the Brazilian Woman from which Macabea is categorically, irremediably excluded.

The figure of the Brazilian woman is only one of the important intertextual references of Amaral's film. It is irrelevant that such references may have little to recommend them from the point of view of the director or of the potential spectator of *A hora da estrela.* The issue is that such cultural phenomena exist and provide major sociocultural horizons for the vast majority of urban dwellers, especially as formatted by television, radio, the movies, mass-circulation magazines, and advertising. Indeed, what is especially significant is the manner in which Macabea interacts with popular culture in ways that are substantially different from those of her roommates and other women. Since Amaral is interested in making of Macabea a heavily highlighted icon of rural women who become lost in the urban abyss, Macabea's differences, rather than marking a unique, original subjectivity, can only serve to reinforce her extreme marginalization: if she is memorable at all, it is because of the utterness of her abjection.

Three major manifestations of popular culture in *A hora da estrela* serve as platforms for the iconic characterization of Macabea's abjection. Critical notes on the film have made much of one of them: Macabea's relationship with the radio, which she spends the majority of her time listening to as she lies in her bed. Macabea—surrounded by the voices of her roommates, who, like Glória, scheme for their survival—just stares vacantly off into space as she listens to the radio, which we hear as a voice-over. Radio is an important companion of the isolated, and, unlike television, it is both readily accessible and portable for the relatively poor. We see Macabea listening to music: in one of the most touching moments in the film, on a day when she misses work on the pretext that she has a dentist's appointment, alone in the room she shares with other women, she fashions herself a wedding veil out of a sheet and dances to classical music, a desperate Sarah Bernhardt. She is almost interrupted by her landlady, who wants to know what is going on behind the closed door and can only barely make out Macabea's moving form through the marbled glass. Perhaps for the first time in her life, and thanks to the radio, Macabea has been provided with some sort of true expressive liberty, unencumbered by the presence of others.

But most of the time, the radio provides a disembodied link to the "real" world. Macabea listens to Rádio Relógio, a station that continually gives the exact time, as though somehow that could be of use to an alienated listener like Macabea. The metronomic quality of these announcements punctuates useless bits of information, program fillers that Macabea, with no real affective tie to the world around her, uses in her attempts to communicate with her roommates, with Glória, and with Olímpico. That there is no communication—neither via the radio nor via human intercourse—is vividly demonstrated by the way in which she tries to involve Olímpico in her attempts to process the information she has heard on the radio. His masculine pride is offended by not being able to understand what she is talking about and by not being able to answer her insistent questions, and he exerts his male prerogative to tell her that these are not appropriate things for decent women to concern themselves with.

A recent article published in a São Paulo newspaper on the "radio girls" demonstrates how exact Amaral's metonymic characterization of Macabea's isolation is. Many of these girls are physically cut off from the world, kept at home to perform domestic chores for working parents or husbands/lovers, doing housework for other women (although in this case the middle-class household's television may serve as company), or executing some sort of piecemeal work on their own. Many of them may be stuck out in rural hovels in urban slums. But many of them may also be like Macabea: as isolated in the midst of the urban cacophony as though she were lost in the middle of the Nordeste desert. Radio provides a multiplicity of programming, and it is interesting to note the sort of station that attracts Macabea. Most women of her class probably listen to popular music (a good amount of which is American, with incomprehensible lyrics, demonstrating that lyrics don't much matter anyway), and Macabea's choice of this particular station may serve to indicate that she is not, after all, as stupid as her appearance suggests. As inane as the programming is, it provides the construction of meaning in the film with a secure point of reference to underscore the tenuous bases of communication for Macabea's universe.

The second popular culture text in *A hora da estrela* is romantic love. Although we do not see Macabea spending much time reading romance story publications, movie and television fanzines, or low-class picture magazines that feature the personal lives of the rich and famous, her roommates read them and discuss the contents out loud, as well as sharing anecdotes about their own love lives. It is clear that Macabea takes up with Olímpico because she wants to have a love life to share with Glória and with her roommates. Although there is never any indication that the two have sexual relations, Macabea begins to behave like a woman in love, and she follows Glória's example in trying to fix herself up a bit, including taking the big step of buying herself a tube of lipstick and some new clothes (romance, of course, is part of the consumerism that drives the big city: romance requires these products, and these products, in their material qualities and in the ads that tout those qualities, echo the romance narrative).

Glória is a loquacious tutor, and she never ceases to tell Macabea about her own conquests and her philosophy of love and to share with Macabea tips to make her more attractive and successful, even inviting her to her mother's birthday party. Moreover, Macabea hangs on Glória's every word when she speaks on the phone with her lovers (which appears to be a good part of the working day), evidently trying to figure out the structure of Glória's erotic life; she also watches in the corner soda fountain as Glória flirts with the young man who works there. Macabea may be an imperfect, even incompetent, student of romantic love, but her attempts with Olímpico, in addition to simply constituting an effort at human communication, demonstrate her striving to key into the narrative of romantic love. Going to the park and to the zoo with Olímpico, her touching attachment to tropical flowers, which she uses both to adorn her body and to decorate her desk at work (Glória at one point snatches the bouquet from the vase, a prefiguration of how she will also snatch Olímpico from Macabea), and going for a walk or a picnic with Olímpico are all details of the romantic narrative. On these walks, during which the urban landscape appears as an anonymous backdrop that marks their marginal presence in it, Olímpico talks and Macabea listens, reproducing assigned gender roles: as marginal as Olímpico may be in the city, his social position is superior to Macabea's. When Macabea does attempt to express herself, Olímpico shuts her up, as when she says that she would like to be an actress. He, who is notably repulsive, ridicules her, asking her if she's running a fever, since she can't possibly think she has the face or the body of an actress (this is an ironic touch, since it is precisely Cartaxo's physical attributes that make her an ideal actress for this film).

The futility of Macabea's romantic efforts is best suggested not by her loss of Olímpico, since she never really appears to have laid any significant claim to him, but rather by her vain attempt to flirt with a man at the soda fountain, only to learn that the dark glasses he is wearing are not a sexually charged detail but rather derive from the fact that he is blind. When he picks up his cane to make his way out the door, Macabea's timid but flirtatious smile crumbles. This is another very cruel moment in the film, but it is a cruelty that marks the urban space. Another scene, less cruel than pathetic, takes place on a subway platform. Macabea believes that a man is looking at her legs, and she looks nervously expectant when he approaches her. But he only advises her, in fulfillment of his duties as a security officer, that she must stand behind the yellow line. Urban romance—and the movie insists on how the attempt to find love depends on details of the urban space, such as scenarios (e.g., parks, zoos) and products (e.g., lipstick, magazines)—intersects with Macabea's exploration of the city. She likes to ride the subway and to observe the passengers; in one scene, she is jammed in between two men who are discussing soccer, and her inquisitive and perhaps even erotically charged gaze is framed by the arc of a tanktop-wearing man's arm and shoulder and the tuft of his hairy armpit.

The third example of popular culture to drive the film is the fortuneteller. Astrology remains strong in all Western societies, and that strength perhaps bespeaks the fissures in the execution of the project of modernity, in which so-called scientific knowledge, even in daily life, is important for the functioning of the machinery (literal and metaphoric) of society and for determining and controlling the orderly consumption of the products of a modern society. A postmodern intellectual skepticism about the efficacy of modern medicine, for example, is less deleterious to the medical industry (because it involves fewer individuals) than a premodern refusal to turn to medicine (assuming always that there is some level of access for the impoverished masses) while continuing to adhere to what medicine views as a superstitious folk medicine. Of course, there is another way to view the remnants of premodern knowledge within the bosom of modernity (no matter how imperfectly achieved in, say, the urban space of São Paulo, the capital of modernity in Brazil): unscientific knowledge is promoted for the masses, a variant of other opiates offered to them, in order to impede and disrupt any understanding of how things really work (more on this below).

Glória turns first to cartomancy because of her frustrations in love, and the fortuneteller (who tells an interesting story about her former life as a prostitute) gives her instructions that will enable her to win the man of her desires. The ludicrousness of all this for the putatively thoroughly modern spectator is the quality of Glória's trivial aspirations, as even she will quickly realize how insignificant a prize Olímpico is. But, then, for Glória the pleasure appears to lie in the hunt and not the game, in the quest and not the beast. Glória convinces Macabea to consult the fortuneteller as part of her own dealings with the woman and on the pretext of helping her. In reality, the fortuneteller has instructed Glória that in order to succeed with men she needs to steal the sweetheart of a friend—hence her interest in Macabea's grotesque Olímpico, and hence her prompt dropping of him when she thinks the fortuneteller's formula has done its magic with a new man.

For the first time in the film, Macabea laughs openly and displays a frank and unreserved smile. The fortuneteller, perhaps also taking pity on her sad-sack qualities, evokes for her an involved tale of romance fulfilled in the arms of a gorgeous man. This prognostication is intercut with scenes of the impeccably dressed upper-class man who will run her down, moving about his rural estate with his race horses in the background. As he climbs into his expensive foreign-model sports car, Macabea descends the stairs from the fortuneteller's rooms to live the gift of illusion that has been given to her. She goes into a store to buy an airy springtime dress, and then she steps out into the street to meet her promised man, who bears down upon her in his speeding car. The star that the fortuneteller has told Macabea will come into her life turns out to be the Mercedes-Benz symbol, on which the camera focuses as the car zooms down the street after the collision. After the man has struck Macabea, he goes back to the scene: the camera follows the line of his sight as he looks down on her smiling and peaceful face. The fortuneteller's cards and her crystal ball have, after all, done their magic.

The cartomancy sequence is the most explicitly developed of the three instances of popular culture in the film, and, as the culminating one, it affirms Amaral's vision: women like Macabea are completely adrift in the urban landscape and the only explanatory narratives available to them are not simply useless for meeting their physical and spiritual needs, but are in fact deadly. Macabea's absorption by the fortuneteller's fabrication leads directly to her death. Significantly, cartomancy's narrative is the one most personalized for Macabea, not just because of the personal interest Glória and the fortuneteller appear to take in her. In contrast to the chaotic narratives of the radio (where there never seems to be any rhyme or reasons for what gets presented, with no basis in the needs of daily life or in what is specifically useful because it is Brazilian) and the impersonal nature of the romance story (by definition, a narrative to which it is understood one and all will wish to adhere, irrespective of personal differences), the illusion evoked by the stereotypical gypsy hag is specifically tailored to Macabea: for the first time she is possessed by liberating joy. Once again, the film is pointedly cruel, with the juxtaposition of the illusion and the facts of Macabea's violent death, but it is the final cruelty.

One of the dimensions of the cruelty of Amaral's narrative is the way in which it forces the spectator to witness the futility of Macabea's life, the life of a woman the spectator would not even deign to recognize, not even be able to discern, on the streets of São Paulo. This cruelty is a particularly insistent correlative of the feminist content of her film.

It has been claimed that there is nothing particularly political about Amaral's film, but I would like to disagree emphatically with such a view. In the first place, her film is political in the general way in which it narrates the trivialized existence of the urban dweller, an existence that is even more trivialized if she is one of the millions of the masses of immigrants who arrive in the big city from the poorest regions of the country. Unless one is willing to maintain that there is nothing significant to say about these people or that this is merely the way things are or are supposed to be, such a narration cannot help but constitute a denunciation. Macabea participates in a socioeconomic dynamic: as I have maintained above, the workings of São Paulo would cease were it not for the dronelike labor of meager wage-earners like Macabea, and the story of someone like her is in a very direct way an interpretation of the system in which she is irretrievably enmeshed. The man who runs her down is both the owner and the most immediate beneficiary of that system. Amaral could have had Macabea run down by anyone, or she could have had her fall into an open construction pit, as she twirls down the street lost in her romantic reverie. That the man is both the paradigm of the perfect lover and a man of importance (because television, magazines, and popular movies make the perfect lover co-terminous with the equally unobtainable exemplars of the privileged elite) is quite an explicitly political statement. One might also note that Mercedes-Benz evokes the white Germanic, Aryan, even Nazi, culture that legitimates the exploitation and extermination of those considered to belong to the "darker" races.

Second, Amaral's film is a feminist document because it tells the story of a woman's life. Let us dismiss any idea that when a woman's story is told, it is the same as telling a man's story. Only when men and women are on the same footing as social actors will such an affirmation make any sense. It is obvious how, as a male social actor clinging precariously to the edge of the urban abyss, Olímpico represents an immigrant without hope or promise, just as Macabea does. However, their different social status is important in the constellation of the masses within which they move: Olímpico may visit his marginalization and his frustration on Macabea. The woman's body (he physically abuses her) and her soul (he ridicules her) is always at the service of the man in a way that can virtually never be reciprocated (cf. the hilarious *Romance de uma empregada* [Story of a Maid, 1988], directed by Bruno Barreto and starring Bety Faria, as an example of how a woman, in her determination to survive, can enjoy the luxury of humiliating both her drunken husband and her lecherous lover). This gross disparity in the nature of social agency among even those who are on the fringes of the urban landscape translates into a feminist perspective, if only of an oblique sort.

Amaral's film is more actively feminist in the explicit way in which it analyzes the construction of different women's lives: the hypocritical landlady, who as a widow must exploit working-class women in order to survive herself; insignificant female employees who must lie to their bosses in order to have a couple of hours to themselves; single women who must live without scruples in order to defend themselves against an urban monster personified by the male, despite being an utter nonentity, as with Olímpico, or by the man of privilege, despite the fact that he was honorable enough to go to his victim's assistance; sexual huntresses, who, in the end, are just as frustrated as any woman in the futile attempt to live the masculinist-based love story. Women are at the core of Amaral's film, and they are women who move in the urban space defined and controlled by masculine privilege: we repeatedly see Macabea striving as best she can to satisfy her male bosses, who, although they take some measure of pity on her, are willing to retain her only because she will work for the minimum wage. These women have no chance of being social agents in any meaningful sense of being in control of their own lives. Of course, there are men in the city as badly off as the women are, and some are perhaps even worse off (male transvestites and male prostitutes, for example; see Perlongher, *O negócio do michê*). But men always enjoy a masculine privilege that women do not, which is precisely why Macabea is Olímpico's scapegoat and not the other way around. Furthermore, a woman whose story is told in conformance with documentary, sociological fact rather than as a figure in a male fantasy (cf. the typical classical Hollywood film: Charles Vidor's *Gilda* [1946]—which comes to mind because of its South American setting—and thousands more) is the protagonist of a feminist narrative precisely because of the measurable difference between the story told here and the one that would be told by a masculinist narrative.

Finally, Amaral's film is political in a third sense because it contradicts the narratives of facile social solutions. As I have indicated, by contrast to Diegues's *Xica da Silva* (in its own way, a masculinist fantasy), *A hora da estrela* sees no sociopolitical benefit deriving from Brazil's return to constitutional democracy in 1985. The external trappings of tyranny made their definitive disappearance, but the new institutionalization of government changes nothing for the likes of Macabea, or for Glória and the former's roommates, for that matter, just as the neoliberalist policies that took effect in the early 1990s (which were confirmed by the dollarization of the economy in 1995)—although they may have meant the greater availability of foreign, including highly visible American, products—are not likely to last long enough or to reach down far enough to make life any easier for Macabea and other internal immigrants. Indeed, one of the greatest ironies of whatever prosperity does consolidate itself is the rush of the impoverished toward that prosperity in the hopes of participating in it; hence the enormous in-migration for a city like Curitiba ("The Brazil That Worked") or rings of shanty towns around the modernist dream city, Brasília (the built-in poverty of Brasília is examined in Wladimir Carvalho's 1992 documentary, *Conterrâneos velhos de guerra* [Old War Buddies]). The millennial abject misery of Macabea, the falseness of the illusion of romantic love given to her, and her eventual death at the hands of a representative of the "owners of the earth" are all cruel political realities that Amaral relentlessly narrates in her film.

Patrícia Galvão (1910–1962) has the dubious honor of being the first woman to be imprisoned in Brazil for her political beliefs and activities. Pagu joined the Communist Party in 1931 (see Dulles, *Brazilian Communism*, 22 and passim). Although from a middle-class family in Santos, she joined the proletariat in factory work in the 1930s, and in 1933 she published one of the few novels of social realism in Brazilian literature signed by a woman, *Parque industrial*, which appeared under the pseudonym Mara Lobo. Subsequent editions (a facsimile in 1981 and a newly typeset edition, regularizing Pagu's erratic Portuguese, in 1981) and an English translation in 1993 testify to the continuing importance of the novel and of Pagu as a recognized feminist in Brazilian culture. Pagu entered into an erotic relationship with Oswald de Andrade, one of Brazil's most important social activists, and they were involved for several years in a journalism that served the Communist and proletarian cause. Pagu's second longtime relationship, after she was released from prison, was with the newspaper publisher Geraldo Ferraz, who financed the publication of *Parque industrial*, which immediately attracted the attention of mainline critical reviews (see Jackson, "Afterword"; Duarte, "Eficácia e limites"; Mafre, "Passeiozinho com Pagu").

Pagu's political activities led her to oppose the authoritarian government of Getúlio Vargas (1930–1945, 1951–1954), which, depending on one's definition of political ideologies, may or may not be appropriately characterized as fascist; it certainly had affinities with the European fascist movements of the period. She had been imprisoned in 1936, and in 1938 the Estado Novo government of Vargas sentenced her to two and a half years in prison. In all, Pagu was imprisoned for a total of four and a half years in this period. Her prison term and the fact that her imprisonment was extended beyond her original sentence for refusing to participate in the ritual greeting of the federal intervenor on his visit to the Casa de Detenção where she was serving out her sentence are part of the legendary aura surrounding her place in Brazilian social history. Pagu is an indispensable part of feminist history in Brazil because of both her intense political activism and her personal status in the São Paulo Bohemian demimonde. Brazilian politics in general passed through an exceptionally turbulent period in the 1930s and 1940s; major cultural centers, and São Paulo in particular, were caldrons of artistic ferment. Indeed, Brazilian culture came of age during this period, and the installation of Modernism with the Semana de Arte Moderna in São Paulo in 1922 is considered the point of origin of modern Brazilian culture.

Pagu is a fascinatingly contradictory figure in that she participated in the worlds of both art and politics: it is important to remember that Pagu always remained firmly anchored in her original class identity. Coming from a middle-class background with a Catholic school upbringing, she had some exposure to culture; first as a decorative woman and then as someone of talent herself, she was able to move with ease in the extremely sophisticated São Paulo scene that derived from the landowning wealth (mostly from coffee and then from industry) that had begun to consolidate itself after the turn of the century. Pagu moved in the world of letters and painting, most of all in the extensive imitation-French café society that segued into the habitués of cabarets catering to the bored and well-to-do. But Pagu also moved in the world of revolutionary fervor. Clearly, the two spheres were bridged by individuals who moved in both: those Communists who claimed to perceive elements of social resistance in a stridently antibourgeois Modernism and those Bohemians who saw their transgression given social meaning in the resistance to fascist and protofascist governments. In this regard, there was a rapprochement—often disclaimed by parties interested in underscoring what separated the two realms—between political revolutionaries and the artistic vanguard in Brazil, as there was also between the Florida and Boedo groups in Buenos Aires (one recalls Jorge Luis Borges's Soviet sympathies in the days of his first vanguard poetry) or the Contemporáneos and partisans of the institutionalized revolution in Mexico.

Pagu as a feminist and as a public figure is an important crossover in the case of São Paulo and Rio de Janeiro circles in the 1930s and 1940s (see Bloch, "Patrícia Galvão"). In a recent survey on Brazilian women's intellectual and cultural models among other women, Marta Suplicy observes: "Observando o destino de

Pagú [*sic*], dá um aperto no coração e uma revolta. Como uma pessoa tão plena de vida e com tal potencial de contribuição pôde ser tão massacrada a ponto de desistir da vida? Questão de mulher? Questão de política? Questão de época?" (Vieira and Giannini, "Super-heroínas").[1]

Norma Bengell's film *Eternamente Pagu* (1987) captures very well Pagu's feminism and her value as a cross-over figure. The film underscores Galvão's resistant and oppositional posture in all realms of life: her transgressions in the temple of decency presided over by the nunlike principal and teachers; her challenges to her father's patriarchal authority and to her mother's passive acceptance of paternal domination; her refusal to be taken only as a decorative woman in the Bohemian world (even when she nevertheless allowed herself the luxury of dressing and conducting herself as a hedonistic Brazilian flapper); her defiance of the masculinist domination of the art world and her alliance with truly transgressive women (the film makes a point of illustrating Pagu's lesbian experiences); her opposition to political authority, which not only landed her in prison but got her prison sentence extended for insubordination; her equal opposition to verticalist party authority, which got her accused of being a willful, personalist woman rather than an obedient comrade. Finally, there is her scandalous behavior as a disrespectful wife to her husband (a marriage of convenience that lasted only from 1929 to 1930) and her insistence on independence in her relationship (1930) with Oswald de Andrade, from whom she separated in 1935, and Geraldo Ferraz, a relationship that lasted from 1940 (from the time of her release from prison) until her death at the end of 1962. It is also apparent that Pagu enjoyed a number of other sexual relationships that probably included other women and, during her trip to Europe in support of proletarian movements there, she had a fling with a French actor named Jean, according to the film.

Bengell's film makes use of material drawn from Pagu's writings and from the abundant material gathered from diverse sources included in Augusto de Campos's 1982 biography and anthology of her writing. Campos has prepared a detailed chronology of Pagu's life (*Pagu*), enhanced by quotes from period sources that indicate the extent of her public persona at a time when few women were able to defy the profoundly overdetermined authority of the Brazilian patriarchy. Indeed, because masculine authority was so strong in Brazil during this period, Pagu's feminism, irrespective of exactly how it is to be interpreted in terms of contemporary prevailing models, is particularly eloquent. Concomitantly, the recovery of her life by Campos during the early 1980s, when Brazil was emerging from almost twenty years of military/authoritarian dictatorship, and the interest in making a film on her during the first year of the return to institutionalism in 1985 are certainly related to her iconic importance on several fronts of Brazilian culture.

This analysis focuses on the feminist dimensions of Bengell's interpretation of Pagu and, by extension, on the feminist qualities that Bengell associates with her historical importance. Bengell, in the person of Carla Camurati (herself a director) as Pagu, engages in a number of strategies peculiar to filmmaking. She is able to use them in an efficient manner that crystallizes the woman's corporal presence in a way not really possible with all of the documentary material presented by Campos, despite the numerous photographs reproduced in his volume. In all fairness, one should note that several of these photographs, such as the one from 1929 on page 302, are especially eloquent. Even though Pagu is in the company of Andrade and friends, this photograph shows her in a very serious and defiant pose; it is possibly the source of the cropped image of Pagu that appears in the film's publicity and on the video box.

Bengell's not very surprising decision to stress the feminist dimensions—as opposed to viewing Pagu, in a typical masculinist fashion, as a social activist who happens to be a woman—has the effect of emphasizing her independence of spirit. This independence got her into as much trouble with the patriarchal universe of her father and its agents as it did with the revolutionary left: both worlds demanded that women be either passive or phallic (i.e., themselves agents of the patriarchy). The Communist movement in Brazil, like the old left anywhere in the West, was unable either to assign agency to a woman qua woman or to cater to any specific woman's point of view. When Pagu was censored in 1931 and forced to proclaim herself to be an "agitadora individual, sensacionalista e inexperiente" (a sensationalist and inexperienced agitator acting on her own: Campos, *Pagu,* 325), she was being obliged to submit to the same sort of patriarchal oppression as she had with her father and with the school authorities (yet Bengell's film makes clear that Pagu's father was never very comfortable in enforcing the Law of the Father: it is he who teaches her to smoke, for example). Where a less feminist interpretation of Pagu's conflicts would range her political activism against established authority, Bengell is concerned with bringing out how on both these fronts, as well in her conflicts (albeit minor) with her first husband and with Oswald de Andrade, she continually faced patriarchal oppression.

Pagu's attempted suicide in 1949 was a culmination of the effects of such conflicts, although it is totally within the spirit of the strength of her character that, by mid-1950, she was deep in a political campaign as a candidate for the Partido Socialista Brasileiro for a seat in the Legislative Assembly of the State of São Paulo. Not surprisingly, she did not win the election, but continued her political and creative activities.

Bengell does not focus on the campaign or on Pagu's subsequent public life. Moreover, the film foreshortens the final decades of her life. She attempted suicide in 1949; in 1962, dying of lung disease, she sought medical advice in Europe. When Pagu was told that her condition was incurable, she once again attempted suicide; she died several months later. Although this point of closure does not distort the accurate representation of Galvão's life, it does serve to emphasize a partial trajectory, one particularly favorable to a feminist interpretation that makes an issue out of the accumulating burden of despair for women in the face of social structures that are as close to absolutely immovable as one could imagine. And, of course, it is more than ironic that Pagu died less than a year and a half before Brazil once again inaugurated a long period of neofascist military dictatorship.

From a cinematographic point of view, Bengell takes full advantage of the opportunities to create a physical presence for Pagu. Camurati is effective in capturing the appearance of Pagu and in transmitting her defiant and rebellious nature, while at the same time underscoring the contradictions between her traits as a well cared for and convent-bred middle-class lady and the physical and psychological demands of factory work, the wear-and-tear of activist politics (street marches, vociferous site protests, even acts of violence and terrorism), and the appalling rigors of incarceration. Conforming on one level to the voyeuristic interest of the camera in the female body, the masculinist gaze that feminist film theory has unstintingly deconstructed, *Eternamente Pagu* specifies the social position of the woman as a social entity under male control. Because of her social background and her creative talent, Pagu can expect something else out of life other than the role of acquiescent helpmeet like her mother. Her grace and beauty provide her an entree into café society and into the Bohemian world, where she meets Oswald de Andrade, usually considered a leader of the São Paulo *modernistas,* and his wife, Tarsila do Amaral, probably the most influential woman artist of the day in Brasil. The initial sequences of the film deal with Pagu's struggles to assert her independent and rebellious nature in school and at home. But the most important sequences are those that follow, about half an hour into the film, in which we see the emergence of her participation in café society and the literary and artistic salons, which leads her away from the sham of her first marriage into her relationship with Andrade.

It is the figure of Pagu as a beautiful and charming nightlife denizen that affirms the basic contradiction of her life and of the struggle for social liberation in Brazil during the 1930s and 1940s. A large number of the revolutionary leaders and spokespersons for entities like the Brazilian Communist Party were themselves of bourgeois origins and continued to lead the sort of cultural life enabled by bourgeois society, no matter how much they felt themselves to be opposed to social convention and no matter how much the avatars of the bourgeoisie felt offended and scandalized by the cultural production of the Bohemians and outraged by their political activism. The scenes of Pagu with her family as a young woman and then as a woman of the world are particularly painful, both in the assertion of paternal authority—and it is clear that her father is basically a decent sort, who may even be uncomfortable with his role as an enforcer—and in the discussions of her political activism and allegedly irregular life. The film is necessarily superficial in some of these regards, and the director opts for a mosaic approach: because Pagu is primarily of interest as a consequence of the intersection between her private life and sociohistorical events, an extensive series of flashes of her relationship to key happenings replaces any attempt at a detailed psychological analysis of her personality. Thus, for example, it is never clear how Pagu comes to be so rebellious and to assume so many audacious and defiant stances toward patriarchal authority. It is enough for the film to show how a beautiful and intelligent woman from a privileged background comes to be Brazil's first female political prisoner.

Of particular importance from a feminist point of view is Pagu's appropriation of symbolic spaces reserved for men; these symbolic spaces are so compact that, no matter what the parameters of political identity may be, there is no room for the direct exercise of symbolic power by a woman. Moreover, whatever symbolic power women have in a thoroughly masculinist society is far from independent or separate; it is, rather, a symbolic power accorded to the social class of "women" by the hegemonic masculinism. This is clear in the film: although Pagu may function as a conventional woman by having a child by Oswald de Andrade, which provides her with the presumed aura of the superiority of woman as the bearer of children, Andrade uses their son Rudá as a pawn in their breakup; and he apparently remains guardian of their child. This of course is particularly true for the period that Pagu will spend in jail. Women in prison, in addition to enduring the punishment that derives from their loss of personal freedom, are also deprived of their symbolic value as mothers, since they are forcibly separated from the children that are conventionally their principal symbolic capital. Pagu does not have a conventional involvement with her child by Andrade, although she is always shown in sincere, loving attitudes with him. She leaves him to make a political trip to Europe, and he seems to disappear from her life. Yet the fact that Pagu does not fulfill a typically maternal role cannot mean that she did not suffer in her separations, whether by choice or imposed, from Rudá.

But Pagu explicitly rejects the crumbs of symbolic capital accorded women in her society; in a period in which it would still have been almost impossible for her to construct an oppositional sphere of symbolic power,[2] she has no choice but to expropriate the elements of masculinist power. Like other revolutionary women of her period—La Pasionaria in Spain or Evita Perón in Argentina—her most effective assertion is not as a feminist in any contemporary sense, but as an agent for the masculinist project. In this case the project at issue is the Communist revolution in Brazil; by virtue of being a member of the so-called weaker sex who is able to execute acts called for by masculine agency, she serves alternately to reinforce the project by being more effective than the men and to put the latter to shame because of her condition as a woman. This is why, like a naughty little girl, she is at one point obliged to confess her inappropriate behavior, which is more characteristic of a willful woman than of a disciplined man.

In general terms Pagu's expropriation of male space is carried out in terms of her political activism, including her candidacy for office at a time when Brazil does not have prominent women in political office, and her literary and journalistic activities. The transition from a relationship with Andrade to Ferraz is particularly important in this regard. Andrade, as a leader of Brazilian Modernism, is nevertheless invested with all of the symbolic power of the bourgeois male. His art may have been in many ways a defiance of academic conventions in its use of vanguard forms, its cultural nationalism (which breaks with the primacy in Brazil of Portuguese models), and its use of themes, particularly those associated with social realism, that break with what the academic tradition considered to be appropriately aesthetic. Yet Andrade remains associated with a Bohemian set still tied to bourgeois privilege; in this sense, as "revolutionary artists," they are only part of the surplus value of capitalism from which most of them draw their roots and which in general supports their art. And, of course, Brazilian Modernism has ended up enshrined as the essence of Brazilian cultural nationalism. Ferraz, by contrast, was much more a member of the proletariat, and Pagu finds with him more of a partnership, which is why their twenty-two-year relationship lasts until her death (see Jackson, "Alienation and Ideology"). Pagu's partnership with Ferraz, despite the fact that she doesn't have a child with him, provides her with her best opportunities to expropriate masculine power: this is the period in which she most maturely participates in the forums of socially symbolic power as a very active public figure. If as a Bohemian Pagu expropriated masculine symbolic power by smoking in public, in cafés, and on the street and by accompanying the men on their rounds, she finds her greatest fulfillment by eventually winning for herself access to the press and other forums of expression as a spokesman for social change in Brazil. And here "spokesman" is the correct word, since Pagu had no choice but to speak for a masculine-identified cause.

Pagu is able to speak in part of women's issues, even if there was no specifically feminist perspective on which to anchor her discourse. Her novel *Parque industrial,* which, as I have said, is the only urban social realist work in Brazil signed by a woman and one of only a handful in all of Latin America, deals almost exclusively with female factory workers, and it undoubtedly draws on Pagu's own experience working in a factory in Rio de Janeiro in 1932. In the novel, in addition to describing the miserable working conditions for women and the slums in which they live, Galvão speaks of various forms of sex-specific exploitation, including the demands by supervisors for sexual favors. She also speaks of the limited avenues of escape from the factory open to these women, such as prostitution, sexual liaison, and, rarely, marriage to a man of better economic standing. Finally, as a trace of the frequently franker nature of Brazilian fiction than is the norm elsewhere in Latin America, *Parque industrial* also addresses the question of lesbian relationships (one will recall that the first Latin American novel to make explicit reference to lesbianism is Aluísio Azevedo's *O cortiço* [1890]; see Reis, "Aluísio Azevedo").

Bengell has obviously drawn on *Parque industrial* for some aspects of her film. Moreover, it is worth noting that she suggests a lesbian relationship between Pagu and Elsie Houston, a Brazilian poet living in France (Houston, who is played in the film by Bengell herself, was married to the French surrealist artist Benjamin Péret). During a visit to Brazil in 1939, Houston visited Pagu in prison. In 1934–1935, during the several months she was in Paris, Pagu resided with Houston, and it is this relationship, with its lesbian overtones, that Bengell presents in the film. Thus, in terms of Pagu's interest in proletarian women's lives and in her relationship with Houston (and earlier with Andrade's wife, the painter Tarsila do Amaral, in whose company Pagu meets Houston in 1929), there is a clear feminist dimension to her persona that I have no intention of underestimating. However, such interests on Pagu's part, no matter how much they may be politically significant to a contemporary feminism that finds Pagu of importance, can have had little resonance fifty or sixty years ago. It is for this reason that emphasis must be placed on Pagu's expropriation of the symbols of masculinist power in order to understand the public importance she had.

This circumstance creates a problem for Bengell's film in the sense that in representing Pagu's life she must necessarily focus on such acts of symbolic expropriation, while at the same time referring, almost as though in passing, to Pagu's more properly (from the contemporary perspective of Pagu as a protofeminist) feminist projections.

I do not know why Bengell does not make more of the possible lesbian nature of Pagu's relationship with Houston or with other women. Perhaps no such relationships ever existed; perhaps the intimacy between Pagu and Houston in the film was no more than what is forthrightly presented. Or perhaps I am not overreading the text and Bengell did mean to imply greater intimacy but drew back from presenting it as such. After all, lesbianism, in addition to being a problem for the essentially heterosexist and often stridently homophobic society of Brazil, still remains a problem for many forms of feminism, which are sensitive to the masculinist irreflexive accusation that all feminists are lesbians (a proposition that, from a radical feminist point of view, is of course precisely the point, although not in the way in which the accusers understand the issue). Whatever the circumstances may be, the fact that *Eternamente Pagu* does not develop in greater detail the specifically feminine spaces of Patrícia Galvão's life leaves the film unfortunately weighted in terms of her struggle for symbolic power with men. Thus, the focal points of the film can only be her suffering in her conflicts with her father, with her comrades, with Andrade, with male prison authorities, and with the circumstances of her attempted suicide in 1949.

Bengell's film suffers in this regard from the difficulties women directors continue to have in making solidly feminist films for a mass audience. If it continues to be true that there is no mass audience for feminist filmmaking in Brazil (a matter that is co-extensive with the problem of finding a mass market for any form of filmmaking by Brazilians, given the enormous weight Hollywood-style pictures have in the national market), a film like *Eternamente Pagu* can only have appeal if it adheres basically to the masculinist historical record. It is for this reason that Pagu's relationship with Andrade must be more important than any relationship she may have had with Houston or Amaral. And it is also for this reason that Pagu's journalism is shown as more important than her novel or her poetry (at one point in the film she claims to have sixty unpublished poems devoted to the subject of censorship) and her relationship with other Communist activists (mostly men) as more important than whatever relationship with other women she must have had during four and a half years in prison.

In 1995 Carla Camurati herself turned to filmmaking. While her *Carlota Joaquina* (on the Spanish noblewoman who becomes the empress of Brazil in the nineteenth century) has much to recommend it for focusing on a female historical figure, the way in which the film undermines official textbook history centers on masculinist history without substituting anything that is specifically about women's lives. In this sense, despite its limitations, *Eternamente Pagu* is much more feminist, especially when one fills in the gaps of Pagu's life from other sources and pursues issues the film suggests but does not explore.

One of the more specifically feminist issues that is handled effectively in the film is Pagu's independence: not just the way in which she senses herself to be an independent person, but the ways in which she is able to conduct herself as such. In the process of pursuing this conduct, she cannot help but challenge masculinist hegemony. The independent woman need not consciously challenge masculinist supremacy, need not overtly identify a man or a group of men as incompetent, in order for her to be the object of suspicion and derision. Rather, the mere assertive presence of a woman in a social setting, with the exception of women who have in special circumstances been delegated voices of authority (e.g., the *grandes dames* of the patriarchy), is enough to threaten the displacement of male authority. Pagu is repeatedly punished for her alleged transgressions. It is significant that these transgressions need not be announced as such either by her or by the agents of patriarchal authority: the authority is assumed to be natural, the transgressions are assumed to be evident, and the application of punishment is assumed to be appropriate.

Although Pagu's independent and often defiant behavior is a challenge to patriarchal authority, that challenge is never defended, not even by Pagu herself, as though such a defense were pointless and as though she perceived that there would be no one there, beyond random voices, to speak in her defense. Significantly, since the film does not establish rhetorically any strategy of defense (except of course for making the effort to show the recurring triangulation of authority-transgression-punishment), it is as though the audience were likewise assuming/to assume that this is the natural order of things in society. We may admire Pagu's defiant manner, but we are not surprised at its consequences, since we may only assume that this is the way things are. Pagu's punishment by her father for defying the nuns, her punishment by both her first husband and Andrade (the first for her unconventional behavior as a wife, the second for being unconventional beyond the bounds of his unconventionality), her humiliation at the hands of Party leaders, her chastisement through imprisonment, and her additional sentence during that imprisonment are all the manifest consequences of her being a bad daughter, a bad wife, a bad lover, a bad mother, a bad comrade, a bad citizen, and a bad prisoner. And since suicide is illegal in Brazil (in addition to being a sin for Catholics, which is Pagu's nominal religion), suicide is not necessarily viewed as a heroic gesture.

Suicide is a common motif in feminist culture, as the ultimate gesture of defiance against control over a woman's body, and it is often seen as a definitive act of self-liberation. It is immaterial what the reasons for suicide are—whether the crushing sense of despair that motivated Pagu's unsuccessful attempt on her own life in 1949 (significantly, by shooting herself in the head, a very "unladylike" and masculine form of suicide), or the refusal to accept the physical suffering from the lung disease that ultimately killed her, or some other motivation. And certainly, because suicide is an extreme measure, a failure in the attempt at suicide can hardly be identified as a failure of will, particularly in terms of the overall risks Pagu took with her body during her lifetime, always exposed to the possibility of fatal violence at the hands of the agents of the patriarchy. Indeed, it is almost incredible that, since we see her being beaten and tortured, she was not raped during her incarceration. Suicide almost always appears to be an unreasonable solution to the living, particularly to those who accept the reasons for proscribing it religiously or legally. Pagu may or may not have known about the suicide in 1941 of the feminist foremother Virginia Woolf, but Bengell certainly would, as would any members of the audience of *Eternamente Pagu* who endorse feminist icons.

Bengell is careful never to present Pagu as a mouthpiece for contemporary feminist standards or for any imagined ideal of feminist behavior. The film always returns, particularly with the constant presence of Pagu's body as a woman in a masculinist society, to the contradictions of her cultural formation and her circle of intensely artistic friends and her proletarian sympathies. Contradictions such as these may have ended up being the bane of leftist politics in Brazil and elsewhere in Latin America: however, they are not Pagu's "fault," but rather the bases of her social formation and the circumstances of her social life. Such contradictions do not nullify any way in which Pagu may have been a feminist activist in her day, nor do they negate the value of her historical figure for a history of women's issues in Brazil. Contemporary feminism is no less fraught with its own contradictions, and it is no easier at the end of the twentieth century to be a feminist (or any other sort of social iconoclast) in Brazil today than it was fifty or seventy years ago.

Except for possibly attempting to demonstrate that *Eternamente Pagu* is disingenuous or ideologically specious (such an attempt would surely fail), there is little point in gauging how successful Bengell's film is as a feminist cultural product. That must surely depend on what one believes feminist cultural production ought to do, beyond providing an intelligent and probing assessment of women's lives. In that sense, *Eternamente Pagu* does meet at least this minimum feminist imperative. When one considers how little filmmaking there has been by women in Latin America (particularly in terms of feature-length films; there has been some record of documentaries), and how much remains to be done with respect to women's history in film, in narrative, or in academic scholarship, Bengell's film is a most respectable entry.

The film opens and closes with Pagu addressing the audience, but in an indirect manner. In the opening sequences, she is walking along the Viaduto do Chá, the famous pedestrian bridge in downtown São Paulo; at the end of the film, after her suicide attempt, she is walking along the waterfront. In both cases a voice-over articulates a series of her meditations on her political and feminist commitments and the need to live a life with the windows open. Finally, the film closes with a text that moves across the screen, to the effect that people should go read about Tarzan, so they can understand what adventure, discovery, and audacity are all about.

Que bom te ver viva

Torture is of particular social significance because it constitutes such a total control of the body by the agents of the state. Whether used as a strategy of interrogation or as a means of discipline, torture involves an invasion of the body in ways that render the victim helpless to counter the control being exercised by the torturer. Torture, unlike many other forms of pain, cannot be resisted, and the history of torture has been the development of physical as well as psychological techniques to ensure that the application of torture cannot be evaded or countered.

Although torture is customarily understood to be a dimension of institutional police power, it is also clear that it has ramifications in everyday life as a displacement or delegation of institutional power in the name of social control. Thus, for example, many now believe that physical violence against children in the name of upbringing (whether by parents or by those who stand in the place of parents such as school officials) is a form of state-sanctioned torture, as is the hazing that takes place in historically homosocial entities such as fraternities and military installations in the name of training and group solidarity. Finally, it has been argued that rape also constitutes a form of torture, especially when rape is viewed as a practice designed to ensure social conformity, whether directed against women (as it almost exclusively is) or directed against men as a confirmation of their status as homosexual subjects (concerning torture in Brazil, see *Brasil: Nunca mais,* which contains a chapter on women and children; see also Allodi, "Women as Torture Victims"; and Sipple, "Terrorist Acts").

While women may rape men or other women, rape is overwhelmingly conducted by men against women or other men, which is why feminist theorizing about rape has tended to view it as a practice legitimated by the patriarchy against those who are viewed as conducting themselves as social subjects in a deviant and therefore correctable manner: women who exceed the bounds of female propriety (hence the abiding belief that rape victims were "asking for it") or men who are insufficiently masculine. It is important to note that with rape, as often with torture as a political event, the circumstances of the event are as significant as how it is perceived by society at large. The individual rapist, therefore, may not necessarily intend to make a point in the name of patriarchal authority, but what happens to the victim may be interpreted both as the assertion of the rights of men over the bodies of women and as the confirmation of the deviance of the victim such that s/he was available for rape. Likewise, individuals may be tortured for many different political and circumstantial reasons—sometimes less for direct reasons of state than on the whim, perhaps erotic, of the torturer. But the victims of torture are often perceived as having deserved to be tortured ("There must have been some reason"), and torture can be perceived, like incarceration and the application of the death penalty, as the legitimate exercise of power by the state in the name of social integrity.

It is for these reasons that the coincidence of rape and political torture—that is, the use of rape as a form of torture—is especially significant, since it concerns the overlap between two such highly socially significant assaults on the body. Lúcia Murat's *Que bom te ver viva* (1989) was produced twenty-five years after the first of the neofascist military dictatorships that were to become, by the mid-1970s, the political norm for the majority of Latin American citizens. The Brazilian dictatorship was also the longest, lasting from April 1964 to March 1985, with torture lasting at least until the end of the 1970s or the early 1980s. A common thread among the neofascist dictatorships was to supplement the routine use of torture for virtually all political prisoners with the intent to extract information about subversive activities and revolutionary groups. In Argentina, and probably elsewhere, Jews were also singled out because they were assumed to be less patriotic as well as unsupportive of the "Catholic" values the regime alleged to endorse. The Brazilian military regime did not have a specific program directed at the elimination of homosexuals. But, given the level of homophobia that still exists in Brazil (as described by Luiz Mott, "Brazil"), it is difficult to doubt that torture in the name of antisubversion included additional attention for women and men who were perceived to be homosexuals or were accused of homosexuality as part of their degradation as legitimate social subjects, to justify their torture.

Murat's film is neither a narrative, strictly speaking, nor a documentary; indeed, one could make much of its hybrid nature as exemplifying a certain type of feminist cultural production where conventional forms are inadequate and hybridness provides greater interpretive opportunities for the social text being examined. This is especially true because one of the recurring motifs in *Que bom te ver viva* is the very feminist issue of the silencing of women's voices.

Que bom te ver viva is hybrid in the sense that it intertwines what can properly be called a documentary with a fictional narrative text (concerning the importance of documentary filmmaking in Latin America, see Burton, *The Social Documentary*).[3] The documentary footage is a series of interviews, accompanied by still footage and material from archival sources, with eight women who were imprisoned by the military during the persecution of political activity in the 1960s and 1970s. Basically, all are professional women (several are university professors) and as a result have given much thought to their experience and how to verbalize it. They are able to provide extensive analyses of their relations with their children and their partners (both those from before their incarceration and those with whom they have made their lives since) and to comment in detail on the relationship between their personal experience, political activism in Brazil, and the military dictatorship and the prison apparatus and, in very eloquent ways, on the feminist implications of their experiences. The need to attain a level of discursive eloquence perhaps explains why the women are drawn from the middle class, with no reference to or inclusion of working-class women, who, in addition to the double marginalization of being political activists/women, also manifest the third degree of marginalization, of social class. Moreover, since the women involved come from urban areas, a fourth element of marginalization—that drawn along the axis of metropolis/province—is also absent. Finally, the women are also marked by their status as mothers and by the importance of their relationship to their children, in some cases in the context of having seen their marriages dissolve as a consequence of the psychological scars of their imprisonment. This overdetermination of the social status of women as wives and mothers also limits considerably the scope of *Que bom te ver viva*. Indeed, one would like to know what might have been the fortune in the hands of the state apparatus of repression of women unmarked or marked negatively by the heterosexist and reproductive privilege—nuns and lesbians.

There are no real surprises in Murat's film in this regard, and in fact the details of the women's abuse, while grim as they can only be, are not really abundant. The viewer mostly fills in on the basis of knowledge from the many published reports now available from both Brazilians and outsiders like Amnesty International about treatment in the country's political prisons. A ground-zero assumption is that the women were tortured and that there is an inevitable sexual dimension to their torture, as there is an inevitable sexual dimension to all torture because of the intimate contact with the body of the other without any of the mediating depersonalization (and, therefore, de-eroticization) involved in medical examination and treatment (concerning torture as a form of female sexual slavery, see Bunster, "The Torture of Women"). Torture cannot but involve the sexual organs because of their extreme sensitivity, and the way in which the entire body can be eroticized in "normal" sexual relations allows for any part of the body also to be eroticized in the application of torture. Moreover, since one can assume that the torturers were all men

(I have found no reference in the large body of writing that there were any female torturers, although there were, of course, notorious examples in Nazi Germany), conventional heterosexist assumptions about men's sexual interest in women's bodies constitute an unavoidable backdrop for understanding the experiences of these women. Surely, there were torturers who could be sexually impersonal about the women's bodies under their hands, beyond the considerations of the likelihood of homosexual torturers who may or may not, in nonconformance with popular myths, have found women's bodies uninteresting or even repulsive.

All of these possibilities feed into the way in which the torture of women prisoners is a manifestation of displaced rape. Actual rape did frequently occur, both as a form of torture and as humiliation of the prisoner because of the manner in which the rape took place or because it took place in the presence of third parties and as a form of abuse separate from the official circumstances of torture.

The way in which the military tyranny justified its existence by touting an ideology of patriarchal affirmation—the defense of the fatherland and of the sacred Western, Catholic traditions of the family—echoes the understanding of all manifestations of rape as the patriarchy's most brutal way of controlling the bodies of women and those, like homosexuals and other marginal groups, who are feminized and therefore made available to the practices of enforcement. One may not accept as unalloyed truth that rape outside official institutional structures, as opposed to rape as integral to political torture, is always the violent side of patriarchal enforcement. But it is imperative, in the context of the use of torture by neofascist governments like post-1964 Brazil, to understand that rape was integral to the enforcement of military dictatorship. The armed forces in power defined themselves in terms of patriarchal privilege, beginning with the mere fact that the government was in the hands of an institution made up exclusively of men who publicly endorsed a univocal masculinist ideology.

There is a statement by feminist scholar Donna Haraway to the effect that "bodies are maps of power and identity" (quoted by Pile, *The Body and the City,* 175, n. 1), and this is nowhere more apparent than in the case of the victims of political torture. If these victims have been chosen for imprisonment, torture, and often death for what is perceived to be their threat to the institutional state, the subjection of their bodies to torture is, as in the case of the machine in Franz Kafka's famous story "In the Penal Colony," an inscription on the body of traces of the power of the institutional state. Moreover, as Hernán Valdés asserts in his memoir of his experiences in the Chilean concentration camp Tejas Verdes following the 1973 neofascist coup in that country (*Tejas Verdes*), the victim of torture is meant to remain as a walking embodiment of the power of the state and as a reminder to the citizenry that the victim may rejoin of what the consequences of political deviation may be (see the analysis of this text by Foster, "Latin American Documentary Narrative").

The former political prisoners—and these are the individuals Murat interviews—are released back into society with profound emotional scars if not physical ones. Indeed, it is almost exclusively of the emotional scars that these women speak, and of the way in which their lives have been radically altered by their experiences. It is significant to note that several speak of losing their male partners as the result of how changed they were by torture, and this emphasis on their relations with men cannot escape a correlation with the fact that they were imprisoned and tortured by men. It is not that their partners are somehow complicitous with the agents of the military regime, although some version of feminism might well maintain such a strong position. But what is undeniable is that abuse at the hands of male tortures is complemented by the inability of their male partners to understand what they have gone through—or, if they do understand it, to come to terms with the way in which it has changed their female partners. Although lesbianism is never mentioned in the documentary, nor any form of female-female bonding, several of the women have gone it alone in a society that places an enormous premium on women enjoying a relationship with a man, and this itself is a repudiation of a significant patriarchal demand.

Murat's documentary segments are framed by a narrative, based on historical fact, in which the actress Irene Ravache plays a former prisoner (who also lives alone) who essentially creates a performance piece in which she reacts to a newspaper interview with a former torturer. Ravache's piece is not included as a single block, but is interwoven with the personal testimonies, which are themselves fragmented in a mosaic fashion. This allows for her angry diatribe, addressed to the camera as though she were addressing the male world of the newspaper and the former state apparatus (even when the director is a woman and women spectators will actually be the recipients of her words), to echo statements made by the former prisoners. This is especially evident in terms of the issue of the silencing of women. Imprisonment and torture, with or without death, is a categorical form of silencing, and the catatonia induced in many prisoners is a concrete manifestation that the apparatus of repression has accomplished its goal (see Diane Sipple's excellent analysis of invisibility and women's place in Brazilian society, "Terrorist Acts," esp. 81ff.).

But the silencing of women and other subalterns is an everyday occurrence, and it plays a prominent role in *Que bom te ver viva*. Silencing takes place by denying the opportunity to speak, by distorting what a woman is able to say when provided with an opportunity to speak, and by refuting or repudiating what she has to say. In the case of Ravache's character, she has been silenced because the paper has reported on an interview that is falsely attributed to her: she herself has had no opportunity to speak, and she is certain that she will have no forum in which to contradict the interview. She speaks of not being able to express herself to her male companion; even when we are the recipients of her diatribe, within the world of the film, she is actually speaking only to herself, exteriorizing her anger but without any interlocutor present to receive her words: there is no one to hear a woman speak. Concomitantly, one of the former real-life prisoners considers the way in which she has been told that it is better to leave such matters in the past, that there is no point in continuing to speak about them, and that, in fact, there is now a new generation of Brazilians who have no direct knowledge of the military regime and the practice of torture, which had essentially ceased a decade prior to Murat's filming.

Finally, *Que bom te ver viva* is in essence a document that exists to contradict and repudiate the strategies of silence applied by masculinist society. There is not exactly an abundance of cultural documents about the experience of torture in Brazil—nor, for that matter, elsewhere in Latin America—during the neofascist dictatorship (see, however, the appendix to the script of Costa-Gavras's film *State of Siege;* although the film is on the Uruguayan Tupamaros, the appendix refers to torture in Brazil). Even a film like Sérgio Rezende's *Lamarca,* while it includes jolting graphic footage about political torture, shows only a man being tortured; indeed, Lamarca's female comrade-in-arms commits suicide rather than give herself up to the police, fully aware of the abuse awaiting her as a woman. The title *Que bom te ver viva* alludes, of course, to surviving with one's life, but certainly not to surviving torture, because Murat's interviewees make it abundantly clear that they will never cease to be recovering ex-prisoners.

Que bom te ver viva functions effectively as a political—and, indeed, as an ideological—document. Produced only a few years after the transition from military dictatorship to constitutional democracy—and in a climate that included specific guarantees for women (such as the famous women-only police precincts)—Murat's film underscores, if only by implication, the ability to speak out that has been restored by the return to democracy. Furthermore, to the extent that military dictatorship is quintessentially a paragon of masculinist authoritarianism, part of the rhetorical effect of Murat's film, as is also the case of the filmmaking in general by women after 1985, is that woman's voice, and especially the doubly marginalized voice of the female political prisoner, is iconic of the juxtaposition of tyranny and liberty, of silence and speaking, that is the organizing principle of *Que bom te ver viva.*

Bananas Is My Business

Carmen Miranda was always struggling to mediate U.S. ignorance regarding Latin American culture, even while she was, in the end, collaborating with the perpetuation of that ignorance. Helena Solberg and David Meyer's documentary on Miranda describes the considerable skill with which she was able to negotiate the Hollywood star system: she is reputed to have told the almighty Darryl Zanuck on one occasion when he balked at letting her have her own way that, unless he acceded to her requests, she would adopt an American accent and thereby destroy her zany image that allowed him to make so much money off of her. Solberg and Meyer present this incident as iconic of the profound fissures in Miranda's artistic persona, as indicative of the tragic flaw in the Carmen Miranda that she first created for the Brazilian cultural industry and then, with something like sinister success, transferred to the film, dance hall/nightclub, and later television venues of the burgeoning U.S. popular culture of the period 1935–1955. In this transfer, Miranda served both the interests of Brazil in projecting an international image (important for the growth of American tourism both before and after World War II and for economic investments; see my comments on *Ópera do malandro*) and the interests of the U.S. cultural industry in finding a marketable cultural icon of Latin America, which had become increasingly popular during and after the war.

The fact that Miranda's versions of Brazilian culture provoked angry responses from some Brazilians, who objected to her kooky eroticizations, and the fact that the American public took (was meant to take) her routines as examples of all Latin American culture speak as much to the disingenuousness of the U.S. culture industry as to the pathos of the only role into which Miranda could ever be slotted. In this sense *Bananas Is My Business* is informed by a postcolonial understanding of how Brazil/Latin America came to be interpreted from the base of the cultural industry in the United States and how someone like Miranda could never stand outside the processes of that cultural industry and was, in fact, consumed by it. If there is any tragic dimension to Miranda's artistic persona, it lies in this circumstance, to which the documentary returns over and over again.

Fragmented identity is the principal organizing interpretive feature of *Bananas Is My Business,* which deals with an identity built around the intersection of gender identity and cultural identity. Solberg and Meyer devote a disproportionate (and dangerously dull) long opening segment of their documentary to showing how Miranda was not really or not completely Brazilian. The daughter of Portuguese immigrants, she was actually born in Portugal in 1909 and moved with her parents to Brazil when she was still a small child. The film underscores how her distant family in Portugal and the villagers of her place of origin still claim her as Portuguese, while at the same time her sister, who is interviewed extensively in *Bananas,* is able to insist that Miranda was thoroughly Brazilian. Miranda's fiery green eyes and her honey complexion are repeatedly evoked as the *verde-amarelo* (green-yellow) of the Brazilian flag: Miranda was educated in Brazil, began her career within the very active Brazilian cultural industry (which became increasingly nationalistic with the fascist Estado Novo of Getúlio Vargas in the 1930s), and attained notoriety, first in Brazil, then in New York, and finally in Hollywood, for her unique interpretations of Afro-Brazilian rhythms. Repeated mention is made of the ways in which her iconic images are versions of Bahia peasant women of African slave descent in her body language, the structure of her dance routines, the clothes she wore, especially her hats, and the lyrics of her song routines.

Although Miranda did come to know enough English to sing in that language (she also sang in Spanish, and it is safe to say that for the majority of her U.S. audiences, there was no distinction to be made between Spanish and Portuguese), she always sang with the heavy accent that—as she appeared to have argued convincingly with Zanuck—was the basis of her success. Someone in the film observes that Miranda might as well have sung in Japanese, for all the sense her singing made to her audience. One could add that her lyrics never made much sense in Portuguese to begin with. The important point was that she produced something of a Gestalt cultural image that could be specified as "Latin American" or, when it was particularly necessary (and I repeat that for U.S. audiences that would have been minimally), "Brazilian."

An abiding theme of *Bananas Is My Business* is how Miranda's identity, split as it is between her Portuguese roots and her Brazilian formation, is irreparably destroyed as a consequence of her American experiences, especially as she began to emerge as an U.S. cultural icon (see Davis, review of *Bananas Is My Business,* 1163). Indeed, the opening and closing scenes of the documentary are of her collapsing on the floor, holding a hand mirror, which shatters into innumerable shards as it hits the floor—a sign of how Miranda had, at the time of her death, hit bottom, living a persona that no longer had any personal or sociocultural coherence. Miranda's marriage to David Sebastian was disastrous and abusive. And as César Romero points out in the interview with him, her image had come to be a parody of itself—indeed, it was parodied extensively by others, including, as we see in one clip, Bob Hope (Mickey Rooney and Milton Berle also performed as Miranda, as did even Bugs Bunny).[4] Finally, Miranda was receiving very bad press in Brazil as a sellout: the Solberg and Meyer's film is part of a renewed interest in Miranda as a valued Brazilian cultural phenomenon. Also of interest is Abel Cardoso Júnior's 1978 book on Miranda as a Brazilian singer (*Carmen Miranda*), part of a musicological revindication of her career.

Vargas had returned to power, and the climate in Brazil was ugly. Although Brazil had continued to maintain good commercial and political relations with the United States since World War II, sectors of the cultural industry, and especially of the educated elite, were ill disposed toward the racist images of Latin America in U.S. popular culture, especially in film. Because of the international enthusiasm for American films and their intensive distribution (many would say, imposition) in the cultural marketplace, film ended up being viewed throughout Latin America differently from literature and journalism. And they were even more ill-disposed toward a woman (one cannot rule out a dimension of sexism here) whose routines seemed often more to be ridiculing Latin American culture than representing it: how could the extravagant woman with the funny hat and the even funnier accent be a legitimate ambassadress for Brazilian culture in a society that essentially had no serious interest in Latin American society?

Thus, Solberg and Meyer would have the spectator understand that Miranda had come to occupy a no man's land: repudiated in Brazil, unloved and abused by a husband whose personal sexual drama may have been the reason for his alienation, and now parodied in American popular culture. Miranda's near collapse on the *Jimmy Durante Show*, only to die of cardiac failure the same night in her Beverly Hills mansion, is viewed as virtually psychosomatic, if not suicidal. In a sense Miranda's persona was the consequence of the cultural inauthenticity promoted by the Hollywood system and the U.S. popular cultural industry. One does not have to be an essentialist or a cultural nationalist to understand how Miranda's routines were more interesting the less they had to do with lived Brazilian culture of whatever stripe. The fabrication of a specific cultural image that fed American stereotypes and fantasies and that responded to particular interpretational forces in the context of the draconian racism of the cold-war years encouraged the persona Miranda created. Today one can be fascinated with Miranda as a camp figure (an aspect that Solberg and Meyer do not explore) and can even be entertained by a rereading of her as a gay icon (something else Solberg and Meyer do not touch upon, although it would be interesting to investigate whether her image has any symbolic currency in contemporary gay and queer cultures in Brazil). But these and other current enthusiasms have little to do with how Miranda and Latin American culture were being read in the United States and in cultural frameworks dependent on Hollywood models of a half-century ago.

The other dimension of identity with regard to Miranda that Solberg and Meyer deal with (without ever addressing the questions of a gay/queer inflection) is that of gender. It is significant that in the film there are a series of fantasy sequences performed by the female impersonator Erik Barreto. The scene with which the film opens and closes—Miranda's collapse in her bedroom—is performed by Barreto, as is a sequence that depicts her arrival in New York in 1939 and her initial interviews with the press in which she establishes many of the basis elements of what will be her Brazilian bombshell/Latin American sex symbol/exotic woman with funny English persona throughout the decade and a half that will constitute her U.S. career. Solberg and Meyer understand very well the dynamics of the U.S. cultural marketplace and how the selling of Miranda as an exotic, foreign product had little to do with her origins (real or fantasized by her) or with a personal artistic vision on her part and everything to do with popular culture demands in the United States (although an image of Carmen Miranda decorates the cover of their book *Machos, Mistresses, Madonnas: Contesting the Power of Latin American Gender Imagery,* it is unfortunate that Marit Melhuus and Kristi Anne Stølen do not mention her in the text).

Barreto's role in the film serves to open up the question of Miranda's self-construction as a sexual object. She unquestionably exploited many of the features associated with sexualized women in film and other entertainment media in the United States (and it should be remembered that her stature, although she was actually not very tall, enhanced by the high platform shoes that were one of her trademarks, was in line with that of other impressive women like Barbara Stanwyck, Joan Crawford, and Katharine Hepburn). Miranda exploited physical features that objectify woman as a sex icon like sensuous dancing, the bare midriff, the exaggeratedly defined mouth, and the constant tutti-frutti display of colors that denoted strong tastes and aromas, not to mention the explicit phallic bananas that were, after all, as the title of the film announces, her dominant trademark (cf. the famous dancing bananas sequence, choreographed by Busby Berkeley in the 1943 musical *The Gang's All Here*). The total effect, whether managed by Miranda herself or by others, was that of a fantasy icon of Latin American female sensuousness that was meant to contrast with the decorum demanded of American women in the period (for example by the Hays code in film). As sexualized as an American star might be for purposes of portraying a fallen woman in the emerging film noir (Mary Astor in *The Maltese Falcon*, for example), there was no competing with the extravagantly erotic model of Miranda, and it is clear that her portrayal of the feminine was meant to mark itself off in categorical ways from the representations pursued by other female stars during the period.

Three issues can be raised with respect to Miranda's construction of the feminine. In the first place, it is questionable whether or not she ever attained any significant level of agency. Although she played the role of the spitfire who was always able to win her own way with men, one cannot escape the fact that her self-definition was always in terms of matching her character to that of a man and her demands were always those of the conventionally defined woman: the attributes of costume and luxury and the undying, undivided attentions of a male admirer. In her famous film with Groucho Marx, *Copacabana* (1947), Miranda so overshadows and dominates Marx in order to get her way that he has barely any starring role at all. Martha Gil-Montero (*Brazilian Bombshell*) reports that he took the part only because he was desperate for work and that he told his biographer that he had "played second banana to the fruit on Carmen Miranda's head" (176). Indeed, during one of the few scenes Marx has on his own, he hides in a closet in a dressing room, disguised as one of the Copacabana's dancers, to escape from the police, who are pursuing him for alleged fraud in his contract dealings as Miranda's agent. As they pull the cross-dressed Marx from his hiding spot, one of the police officers says to the other: "They always end up in the closet." This throwaway homophobic allusion only contributes to the diminishment of Marx in his dealings with Miranda as an invincible woman who, indeed, plays two separate parts in the film, thereby doubling her exercise in the construction of the feminine.

Miranda's overconstruction of the feminine, nevertheless, in addition to leading to the mocking caricatures mentioned above, comes, from a semiotic point of view, to burst at the seams. It is so overdetermined, so full of redundancies, so self-referential, and so replete with symbols that lend themselves to problematical interpretations (for example, Busby Berkeley's giant dancing banana sequence in *The Gang's All Here*) that it results in occupying a gender no man's land: Miranda appears to be a woman playing a man playing a woman. If we can understand drag as something other than an imitation of the feminine, and therefore as something other than a mocking putdown of women, it becomes possible to see it as a critical commentary on the construction of the feminine: femininity comes to be portrayed as an articulation of gender imposed on women by the hegemonic sexism of a masculine-dominated society. Thus, when men perform as women they underscore the way that men are, in fact, in control of a standard definition of the feminine; for this reason it is immaterial whether the cross-dressing performer constructs his own gender identity (it is an erroneous generalization to believe that all men who impersonate women are gay, that they are men who want to be women; see Garber, *Vested Interests*). The consequence in Miranda's case is that she becomes after all her own worst caricature, and this is patently obvious as the fetishistic fascination of American culture with the Latin American exotic fades by the end of the 1940s. As Shari Roberts notes:

> Miranda performs a femininity so exaggerated that it becomes comical, undercutting any threat that her female sexuality might pose but also calling into question society's assumptions about feminine essence. Additionally, while Hollywood representations of different ethnicities often draw on, emphasize, and contribute to stereotypical ethnic cliches and myths, Miranda's ethnic persona nears hysteria with its exaggeration. Miranda's costumes lampoon both feminine fashion and traditional and stereotypical Latin dress—stacks of accessories, shoes so high they impede walking, and cornucopia hats. Miranda's outfits suggest female sexuality in excess, revealing and accentuating her sexually invested body parts: the navel, breasts, and legs. ("The Lady in the Tutti-Frutti Hat," 15)

The third issue associated with Miranda's gender construction has to do with her fortunes back in Brazil. As Solberg points out, Miranda found to her dismay that Brazilians were not always enthusiastic about her success in the United States. Although Getúlio Vargas contributed to her move to New York in 1939 (Lee Schubert, who had traveled to Brazil to see if she was worth contracting, was willing to pay for her, but not for her band; Miranda insisted that she could not perform without her band, and Vargas footed the expense for their travel), the way in which Miranda fed a uniquely American fantasy about Latin America, one in which her specific association with Brazil was lost, was disconcerting. Moreover, that fantasy had an unmistakable ugly racism associated with it to the effect that Latin American women are all sexpots, and this interpretation hardly jibed with Brazil's energetic efforts to establish its international importance in the arena following World War II.

When Miranda returned to Brazil in 1954, she was received coldly in official cultural circles (see Gil-Montero, *Brazilian Bombshell*, 236ff.), although popular audiences continued to respond enthusiastically to her performances. The combination of Miranda's representation of Latin sensuality and, perhaps more than anything else, her insistence on the incorporation of black culture motifs at a time when racism continued to be virulent in the United States struck a sensitive nerve in a Brazilian establishment that knew very well that part of the difficulty of its participation in the new world order led by the United States was the perception of Brazil as a country of blacks and mulattos. Thus, not only was Miranda's female sexuality overdetermined in a strictly gendered way, but race (both Indian and black) functioned as a powerful subtext that could simply not be ignored: Miranda was dangerously invoking a motif of nonwhite women as virtual sexual perverts. As one defamatory article mentioned by Gil-Montero states in its headline, Carmen Miranda "should go back to the savages" (224).

Solberg and Meyer's documentary unfortunately does not probe any of these issues of race and gender in any depth. They are basically interested in demonstrating the disintegration of Miranda's personality under the effects of her success in the United States, but it apparently does not occur to them that part of this success was built on a construction of feminine sexuality that was tightly bound up with Brazilian and Latin American identity—and in turn with questions of race—that could have been profitably explored.

One of the particularly successful rhetorical strategies of the film is Solberg's own narrative voice. She begins by telling how her mother had not allowed her to participate in the public spectacle of Miranda's funeral, which included street manifestations and collective expressions of grief, and says that her film is one way of understanding a figure that she felt had eluded her because of her mother's prohibition. This manner of personalizing the director's relationship with her own material is characteristically feminist and breaks with a documentary norm of nonpersonal involvement with the material being reported (see Burton's interview with Solberg in *Cinema and Social Change*, 81–102). As Teresa de Lauretis has argued in her analysis of a woman's cinema that is marked less by feminine content and more by a feminist consciousness vis-à-vis cultural production, it has become important to demonstrate that filmmaking, or any cultural production, is artifice and not a "natural" and transparent privileged window on reality. Culture is a construct, and as such it is mediated interpretation. Thus, she argues that the conditions of that interpretation require encoding into the document itself:

> The novelty of this direct address . . . is not only that it breaks the codes of theatrical illusion and [masculinist] voyeuristic pleasure, but also that it demonstrates that no complicity, no shared discourse, can be established between the woman performer (positioned as image, representation, object) and the male audience (positioned as the controlling gaze); no complicity, that is, outside the codes and rules of the performance. (*Technologies of Gender,* 143)

In this way, Solberg, by bridging the aesthetic distance between herself and her subject and by involving herself in the events she describes, makes Miranda of direct pertinence as a female artist by suggesting a correlation between the two women, which is even more pertinent in view of Solberg's own professional formation in the United States.

Bananas does in fact avoid gender issues in a theoretically grounded way: none of the individuals interviewed on camera refer to Miranda as exemplifying women's history, and Solberg's narrative exposition returns time and again to Miranda as a Brazilian figure, but not as a woman whose pathos is related to the treatment of women by a masculinist society or by a masculinist entertainment industry. In this sense, there is the color of bourgeois uniqueness about Miranda, at least on the level of the film's ideology, and the meaning of Miranda for the experience of women emerges only in a critical reading such as this one. By the same token, my identification of a possible interest from the perspective of drag, while it is more explicit, through the use of a transvestite to represent Miranda at strategic points, still remains an insinuation in the film; it is not clear if the transvestite figure is only a felicitous choice to represent Miranda's exuberant theatrical persona or if there are, in fact, interesting observations to be made about how Miranda constructed a female Brazilian/Latin American identity for U.S. audiences. If Solberg perceives this dimension of Miranda, she never says so in any immediate way.

The most salient feature of the films dealing with the construction of feminine identities, in addition to the simple fact that there is now a group of important women directors in Brazil, is the way in which all five texts are directly contestatorial on the level of the filmic text itself. The interpretive commentary, while it may go against the grain of a film's specific interpretation of women's issues, necessarily begins by recognizing the way in which the film itself is a critical reading of masculine hegemony. In this sense, *Eternamente Pagu* must stand out as the signal film here, for the way in which it deals with a historical figure whose person and writings are rich in feminist dimensions, but also for providing a feminist interpretation of those feminist dimensions. As the first Brazilian woman sentenced to prison for her political activities, Pagu stands as an icon of the way in which the multiple boundaries placed on women are forms of incarceration; one of the most potent segments of the film has to do with the way in which Pagu is censored by the men whose political program she shares.

If Pagu moves immediately to the macropolitical level in the use of a resonant historical figure, *A hora da estrela,* like so much of the best of feminist cultural production, functions on the level of the micropolitical: Macabea, unlike Pagu, can have no conscious realization of the degree to which she represents issues of women's lives in Brazilian society. Of course, the two women are connected in that their lives end tragico-pathetically, but that is hardly surprising in view of the violence to which women are exposed in ways that most of them are not even aware of: what perhaps makes the greatest impact in *A hora da estrela* is that Macabea neither knows what is being done to her nor has even a flash of awareness that she has been run down.

Que bom te ver viva and *Bananas Is My Business* also are divided by the micro-macropolitical axis, although in different ways. Both texts are historical. Miranda, as the first Brazilian woman to become a big international attraction, is shown to be as much a metaphor of the status of Brazilian culture on the international marketplace as of women's difficulties in achieving artistic transcendence. The image of the broken mirror that frames the documentary speaks as much to the individual schizophrenia of the big-name star Carmen Miranda as it does to the fragmented lives of the forgotten women who were the victims of torture during the dictatorship. Miranda continues to be a cultural icon, but these women are forgotten both because they are women and because there is a tendency in Brazil to consign the dictatorship to a period that is now over and done with, an attitude that only serves, in the opinion of the women interviewed, to invalidate the traces of that period that are still written on their bodies.

CHAPTER 3

Same-Sex Positionings and Social Power

*Não de minha filha. Ciúmes de você. Tenho! Desde o
teu namoro, que eu não digo o teu nome. Jurei a mim
mesmo que só diria teu nome a teu cadáver. Quero que
você morra sabendo. O meu ódio é amor.*
—NELSON RODRIGUES, *O beijo no asfalto*[1]

Popular knowledge would have us understand that Brazil is a so-called sex-positive society, an identification that is accompanied by a belief that Brazil is also very open to homoeroticism. Indeed, in comparison with other Latin American societies, Brazilian scholars have produced some important documents concerning same-sex desire (Foster, "Do 'para inglês ver'"). Yet it would be a serious mistake to believe that homophobia is not a profound component of Brazilian culture or that it has only been confined to periods of military rule (as though, somehow, military rule were not an integral part of the country's sociopolitical process). While one can point to important homoerotically marked writings in recent years—the very inventive texts of Glauco Mattoso (see Foster, "Glauco Mattoso"), the memoirs of Fernando Gabeira (see Borim, "Fernando Paulo Nagle Gabeira"), the impressive novel *Risco de vida* (Risks of Life) by Alberto Guzik (1996)—Brazilian popular culture and overall social values continue, nevertheless, to be driven by versions of homophobia.

This chapter examines three widely distributed Brazilian films to see how homophobia, and homophobia's construction of same-

sexuality, is used for purposes of interpreting the Brazilian social text.

Barrela

Plínio Marcos's play *Barrela* had to wait over twenty-five years for
its film version (see Camargo, "Un diálogo constante"; see also the
Hoin review in *Variety*). Although it was written in 1958 and first
staged in Santos in 1959, the intervening military government
made it impossible for it to be either restaged or made into a
movie, and the text was not published until 1976. Like Marcos's
theater in general (see Schoenbach, "Plínio Marcos"), *Barrela*
deals with the correlation between social and interpersonal violence. Violence is a structural property of the dominant social system. Indeed, that system depends on violence as a complex instrument to insure its function: violence is used in the formation of the
social subject; it is used to correct and fine tune the behavior of
the subject in his/her existence within society; and it is used as a
displayed reminder about what the consequences of improper
conduct within the system may be.

Moreover, the violence of the dominant social system—institutional violence—is reduplicated in the interpersonal relations
between social subjects, for whom it may function specifically as
a negotiation not of interpersonal relations, but of the relationship
of one subject in the presence of the other, before the social hegemony. This occurs whether other subjects, with or without a role of
institutional authority, are materially present or are only imagined
to be present in the mind's eye. Marcos's plays are customarily
skeletal microcosms (regrettably, George, *The Modern Brazilian
Stage*, barely mentions Marcos; see the more extensive comments
in Albuquerque, *Violent Acts*, where, unfortunately, *Barrela* is not
mentioned). Of course, all spectacle, particularly theatrical spectacle, functions microcosmically, but the point with Marcos is that
his plays make it clear that his characters have little so-called psychological density and are, despite their superficial individuations
as grotesque figures, entities whose conduct reduplicates with
chilling efficiency and clarity impersonal social dynamics.

Marcos's violence is paradigmatically sexual. This is so, first, because Western society invests sexuality with layers of horror, repugnance, and taboo, as well as because sexuality, as the institutionalization of one of the body's basic needs (erotic desire), conveniently provides one instrument for the application of violence to the subject as part of the triad of formation/correction/reminder. Second, because desire is a basic human need and because it has been invested with such awesome myths, it has come to be viewed as one of the most intimate dimensions of one's subjectivity under the guise of the privacy of the body. Thus, an invasion of that privacy can be especially efficient as a form of overdetermined or multiply effective violence. Finally, the institution of sexuality as such ties erotic desire to a binary of differentiation grounded in the sexual, the genital, and essential social roles. Rape, the name given to violence utilizing the sites and organs of erotic desire (an inventory that cannot be viewed as categorically stable, although sexuality at its most patriarchal may wish us to believe that it is), specializes in the binary of differentiation, and its model is the masculine penetration of the female.

Such penetration utilizes the penis or some bodily substitute (fingers, toes) or extrabodily substitute (dildos or virtually anything that matches the Freudian displacements of the penis), and the feminine is any body into which the penis is inserted, necessarily with as much brutality as possible. The site of the insertion is the vagina or its displacements (any other orifice already in existence or, in some cases, orifices created for the occasion—this is fairly standard feminism; see Dworkin, *Intercourse*). Significantly, this imaginary may involve a male body that is feminized, with any of its orifices, existent or ad hoc, being taken as a substitute for the vagina. The preferred substitute for the vagina in the case of either a woman's body or a man's body is the anus, both because of the extreme pain caused by sudden penetration and, in the case of the male body, because of the anus's role as the traditionally favored site of homoerotic pleasure (not because of the anus as a vagina substitute, but because of the role of the prostate in sexual pleasure). Men thus raped are degraded as "women." One could speculate that the anal rape of women is to signify them as degraded men: in a sexist society, overvalued men are valueless when degraded as women, who are undervalued to begin with.

Marcos's plays do not work on the basis of this sort of textbook explanation of the structure of social violence, the dynamic of sexual brutalization, or the semiosis of rape. But they certainly depend on the way in which we know intuitively that this is precisely how things work. The plays may serve to convert our intuitions into explicit knowledge or to fill in the gaps we may have: first, on the level of intuitive understanding or, second, on the level of what we think we know explicitly, always working off of the theoretical assumption that ideology has worked to conceal or to distort such knowledge for us and that cultural production is necessary as a gesture of unmasking and sorting things out. Since part of the mythic interpretation (in Roland Barthes's sense of the term) of institutionalized sexuality is to conceal as much as possible the nature of erotic desire and what the social hegemony has done with it in the form of institutionalized sexuality, theatrical representations of either erotic desire or sexual violence involve a lot of stress on the part of the majority of audiences. When one adds the possibility that the execution of erotic desire may legitimately involve a sexual theatrics that makes use of signs of sexual violence, things get even more troublesome.

Authoritarian societies, which have the greatest vested interest in keeping the workings of social violence and one of its major tools, torture by sex, hermetically hidden, simply address the matter by banning wholesale anything having to do with sex. The erotic, as one can well imagine, gets banned as such because it may model alternatives to social violence as the basis of interpersonal relationships; and anything having to do with violence is banned when it is grounded in an interpretation of the hegemony, although the representation of violence as an "extraterrestrial" phenomenon (e.g., the work of the devil) or as belonging to "their" society but not "ours" ends up with its representational due (concerning violence and sex under military tyranny, see Graziano, *Divine Violence;* concerning male sexual fantasies and authoritarian violence, see Theweleit, *Male Fantasies*).

Failure, inability, or refusal to grasp the points that have been made so far will result in either bewilderment in the face of Marcos's plays or repudiation of them as nothing more than chaotic filthiness, which was, of course, exactly how military censorship addressed them (see comments by Marcos on the censorship of his plays in Szoka, "The Spirit of Revolution," esp. 76, where he reminds us that his play was banned during the democratic Juscelino Kubitschek government). Since Marcos has devoted himself to the theatrical staging of male-male violence and, in numerous works, to male-male rape, it means that the bulk of his theater was susceptible to denunciation and censorship (on theater censorship in Brazil, see Michalski, *O teatro sob pressão;* Marcos is not discussed). It can only have its full meaning among spectators who have acquired or wish to acquire a complex understanding of the theories of violence and rape on which Marcos grounds his theater, whether that grounding is to come from Marxian social philosophy, radical feminism, or, more recently, queer theory. This is so to the extent that the latter has as its essential component an interpretation of the construction of institutionalized sexuality and the use of same-sex rape as an instrument in the oppression of homoerotic desire.

Marcos's focus on male-male rape is integral to his analysis of the violence that is crucial to social hegemony as he understands it. His theater is not sexist because it represents an almost exclusively male world; nor is it sexist because it portrays the dominant masculinism of that world. Rather, the point must be that our social hegemony is driven by the primacy of those social subjects called "men," and therefore an analysis of those social subjects and the specific ideology of their primacy, masculinism, is in order. Furthermore, since violence is the pedagogy, the metric, the enforcer of masculinism, the execution of that violence must be charted in all of its details, in all of its multiple workings. Finally, to the extent that one of the preferred instruments of that violence is, among men, male-male rape—the more "professional" instruments of torture are not always handy, but a body is always available to rape the body that is the object of attention—Marcos's theater must accord privileged attention to explication of the rape scenario. As we will see in the case of *Barrela,* ensuring that one individual gets raped is the specific goal of police actions.

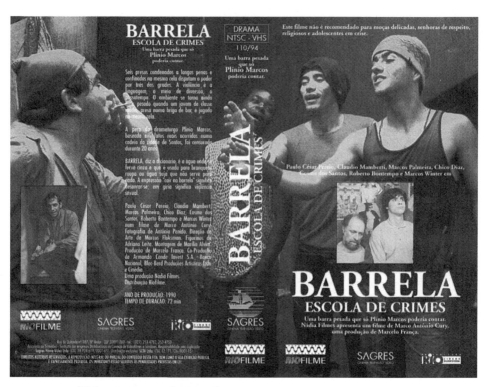

Video promotion for **Barrela**.
Reproduced by permission of Sagres Home Video Ltd.

Cury's film is divided into four movements. The first three are set in a cell containing individuals who have been sentenced for violent crimes (in the play, it is only a holding cell). The fourth movement is set in the corridor stretching from the cell to the exit from the jail. There is a third setting, which is intercut with the jail cell: the interior of a police car transporting a young man across town to the jail. Finally, there is an opening setting which is part of a sexual reverie of one of the individuals sentenced to the cell. *Barrela* recounts the odyssey of a young man, called simply Garoto, in the hands of the police. A handsome middle-class youth, barely more than a boy and wearing a nicely cut pink shirt, is picked up for getting into a fight in a bar. Although Garoto appears approximately halfway into the film, everything leading up to his appearance is prefatory to his relationship with the occupants of the cell, and the spectator soon realizes that he has been tossed in with these prisoners to teach him a lesson. But before discussing that lesson, it is necessary to follow the set-up used by Cury.

The opening sequence of the film is Portuga's reverie concerning the man and woman he has killed. This reverie does not appear in the play, which opens with Portuga's noisy responses to what there is called a nightmare. This sequence, which lasts about ten minutes, is, for most of its duration, a typical clip from a porno film: we see two extremely attractive bodies making love in assorted full-body/full-frontal nudity positions, with accompanying soundtrack. The bed on which they perform is enveloped in a mosquito net, which allows the camera to move from direct shots of their writhing flesh to a softly filtered shot of their reposing bodies. However, the porno film conventions are interrupted, and instead of the requisite so-called money shot (i.e., the man's spurting ejaculation on the body of the woman in order to confirm that "real" sex has, in fact, taken place), we see spurting blood, apparently on a glass screen interposed between the actors and the camera, to signify their being stabbed by an assailant.

It is not clear if it is Portuga murdering them as part of a robbery or as an act of revenge or if, more likely, it is the intersection in his mind between a wet dream and some act of violence for which he has been incarcerated (we do discover later that Portuga is, in fact, serving a sentence for killing an unfaithful wife). What is important is that, when the scene shifts from the horrified faces (attractive, innocent) of the interrupted lovers, we see the fat and slovenly Portuga, an emblem of the filth of a miserable jail cell, mumbling to himself with his hand down the front of his pants. Portuga's nightmarish preorgasmic noise has awakened his companions, and the movie moves into its second sequence, which assumes the form of a visual round (in the musical sense) based on the need to establish authority by dumping on someone else. There is an overlapping repetition of the same structure, which begins each time from a different point in the chain of relationships between the prisoners.

Because Portuga's companions are angry at having been awakened by his grunting and groaning, he becomes the object of the enactment of the game that is called in English Smear the Queer. This game involves singling out one individual in a group and identifying a symbolic weakness. It is immaterial if the individual is singled out first and then the weakness is perceived or if the weakness is strategically perceived first in an individual and then the group decides to pursue it: the cause-and-effect is rather like a semiotic Möbius strip with no discernible before and after. Typically, the symbolic weakness is perceived as signifying a sexual shortcoming, more specifically, something discerned as a sexual deviation. The deviation need not necessarily refer to homosexuality, although that is certainly the most obvious choice. It may also refer to an alleged sexual proclivity that is, if only spontaneously and conveniently for just that moment, seen as unacceptable, as in the case of the sexual molestation of minors in the Nuyorican Miguel Piñero's 1975 play *Short Eyes* (U.S. prison slang for a child molester).

Portuga is harassed by his cell mates, who, egged on by Louco, assure him that they are going to sodomize (*enrabar*) him for having awakened them all with his dream. The logic of violence here has nothing to do with whether Portuga is a conventional candidate for sodomy (i.e., a *bicha,* a queer), but that he may be considered one for the purposes of a moment that demands a discharge of violence as a corrective for having been awakened rudely (as though there were any other way to be awakened in a crowded prison cell). The fact that Portuga is, by conventional definition, the most physically repulsive of the six men underscores that sexual desire is not at issue and that the object of the dramatic act of violence has nothing to do with attributing a sexual identity to him.

Portuga's harassment is interrupted by Bereco, who exercises the authority of cell captain, the individual who has won a measure of allegiance from his companions and who enjoys special privileges among them. Bereco has his own special corner of the cell, which he has curtained off and decorated with a poster centering on soccer and women in sexual poses. He defuses the situation, and it is obvious that he is used to having to do so. Individuals like Bereco (a type of trustee, but one who emerges by consensus of the prisoners because of his ability to impose himself on them) are used in a sense by prison authorities when they cannot maintain sustained vigilance over prisoners, especially in primitively organized institutions. The cell captains receive special consideration in exchange for keeping the violence down. Not for suppressing it, however: Bereco understands very well that the continual welling up of violence must be respected as a necessary ingredient of the social situation in which they all find themselves and that it must be tolerated, permitted, even at times encouraged. But he also understands that it must be controlled, and he has an entire rhetorical arsenal at his disposal to do just that.

So the outburst against Portuga is contained, but the calm is short lived, and the film segues into the next stage of the round of violence. Led by Portuga—the victimized becomes the next victimizer in the harsh and unyielding logic of violence—the cell mates now turn on Tirica. Tirica is the most conventionally attractive of the six, and we learn that in order to survive on the streets, he turned to hustling, to being a *michê* (taxi-boy), capitalizing on a relatively pretty face. Despite Néstor Perlongher's somewhat romantic interpretation of the *michê,* most such male street hustlers are not gay. Although some of their clients may be well-to-do women slumming, in general they are servicemen, tourists, or locals able to pay a fee (Tirica calls them *mandarins*), and, like female prostitutes, the *michês* assume whatever role the client demands. Portuga, of course, is not going to indulge in the social-anthropological distinctions between sexual identities and the roles whores play.

The game of Smear the Queer demands locking on an exploitable weakness. Being a prostitute is not a good one, even if it may be true that male hustlers get less respect than female prostitutes do. Issues of masculinity do seem to be involved in the social perception of male hustling, and—also in part because male hustlers are more often than not asked to adopt an aggressive macho pose—there is a far higher index of crime (robbery, assault, and even murder) by *michês* against their clients than is the case in heterosexual prostitution. Often it is the female prostitute who is the victim of violence at the hands of her client, who may use her to play out a role of aggression which is demanded of him by society but which he cannot thoroughly enact in other venues.

In any case, it is not enough to harass Tirica for being a hustler, so Portuga triumphantly undertakes the rhetorical operation of converting *michê* into *veado,* using Tirica's hustling to claim that he is a queer. This is an effective move: now the hoard turns on Tirica, and Louco once again intones the imperative to smear him, "Enraba." Once again Becero intervenes, not to save Tirica, but to restore order before things get out of control. For the audience, there is a gradation involved here. Portuga is repulsive in appearance, and the spectator is unlikely either to identify with him or to contemplate his body as a fetish, a site for the provocation of sexual desire. Tirica, by contrast, is much more of an acceptable sexual symbol, because he is young, athletic in appearance, and blessed/cursed with a relatively attractive face. Films routinely use actors and actresses who meet conventional definitions of physical beauty and erotic attraction in order to provoke identification on the part of the spectator. Such identification is often "queer," to the extent that the distinction may become tenuous between whether one is identifying with the star, irrespective of one's own sex/sexual identity, and wishing to be a sexual agent like the star or whether one experiences the pull of erotic desire toward that star.

In this sense, stars are essentially androgynous, which is why Hollywood has historically invoked two types that were, outside of film, unacceptable to the "real world" of patriarchal heterosexuality: the strong woman (e.g., Bette Davis) and the beautiful man (e.g., Tyrone Power) (see Doty, *Making Things Perfectly Queer;* Dyer, "There's Something Queer Here"; Bell-Metereau, *Hollywood and Androgyny*). Indeed, it would be difficult to decide which is the greater sin, to be a strong (= masculine) woman or to be a man with a pretty (= feminine) face. But Tirica is a street tough; in the face of his tormentors, he is able to adopt all of the attitudes necessary to defend himself, including contorting his face into an ugly mask of anger that erases the overt metonymy that had helped allow him to be the queer of the moment. If the pure violence associated with harassing Portuga is now more reasonably tinged with some trace of erotic desire in the case of the more conventionally attractive Tirica, Becero makes sure that the aggression against him stops before any major physical contact takes place. Tirica goes off to begin forging a knife from his eating spoon with which he will later stab Portuga to death in retaliation for this public misidentification of him as queer bait. Meanwhile, Garoto arrives.

In terms of the gradation of male attraction from Portuga to Tirica to Garoto, the last is eminently desirable. Again, I am speaking here in terms of certain conventions that can be verified by reference to the stereotypes of television, advertising, and commercial film; these stereotypes in Brazil are not substantively different from those that prevail in the United States for obvious reasons of market dependency. Thus, Garoto is young and clean cut; his clothes are, if not expensive, at least considerably better than the cheap and unkempt clothes of the prisoners he is tossed in with, not to mention the virtual rags worn by Portuga; and his general open-faced manner is that of someone who is accustomed to some sort of consideration from others in life. In addition to fitting the stereotype of middle-class prosperity, Garoto is sexually attractive as a young man: his face is clean shaven, his skin is good, and his hair is professionally cut; he is bright eyed; and his build is slight without being androgynous. More importantly, because his body is not street hardened like that of Tirica, it fails to meet a criterion of hypermasculinity that someone like Tirica (or Fumaça and Bahia, the two other young men in the cell) depends on to protect himself from sexual aggression.

Despite whatever self-identity Garoto may have and despite whatever heterosexual successes he may have with women in his own social milieu, he is immediately tagged as queer bait by the prisoners with whom he is placed. No sooner has the door of the cell closed behind him than he is greeted by all six of the inmates, with Louco again articulating the crucial imperative:

Bereco. Filhinho de papai.
Portuga. Parece uma menina.
Bahia. Garoto bonito.
Tirica. Agora que eu quero ver quem é macho.

Fumaça. Que é? Já está com idéia de jerico pra cima do garoto?
Tirica. Náo está todo mundo na pior? Vamos enrabar ele.
Louco. Enraba, enraba mesmo![2]

Tirica gets two opportunities to speak in this sequence of greetings, as though, because he has been the object of the previous round of Smear the Queer, he gets to single out the new candidate, first by evoking the macho identity and then by putting forth the proposition of gang rape. The first three declarations refer to conditions that detract from Garoto's masculinity, such that he becomes susceptible to the rape of the feminine: (1) his youth—the condition of being a *filhinho de papai* (Daddy's little boy) also has class dimensions, with the proposition that individuals of the middle class are less sexually defined than are those from the lower classes most of the prisoners come from;[3] (2) his delicate physical features, lacking the hardness of Tirica/Fumaça/Bahia, allow him to be categorized as a little girl; and (3) he is good-looking, a fatal flaw, since beauty in a man feminizes him. Playing off these three assertions of sociosexual classification, the next three put forth the proposition of gang rape. Tirica's evocation of the macho (that is, the hypermasculine) declares the contrast between them and Garoto, as well as referring back to when his own masculinity was questioned—now it will be clear that, when compared to Garoto, encoded as a *menina,* there can be no question of Tirica's full condition as a man.

The action moves swiftly on the basis of Louco's repeated command. Cury chooses not to depict the rape as such, and we never see Garoto bared. Rather, the camera pans back, and the scene rotates in a very conventional representation of the vertigo Garoto supposedly feels himself engulfed by, an experience that he probably has heard of but certainly never had. Moreover, references to rape that he may have heard about probably involved young girls who carelessly ended up in compromising situations. He may or may not have heard about the power function of rape in prison, although it would be difficult for him not to, since such circumstances are common knowledge in Brazil as part of the terrifying power the image of prison has to exercise social control. While Cury provides an acceptably conventional representation of the rape itself and avoids any possibility of being accused of sensationalism or pandering to "homosexuality," he does not do a good job of handling the consequences of the rape. In the first place, the camera does not dwell very long on the violated body of Garoto, as though it were not necessary to do much with the psychological consequences of his "feminized" humiliation. Certainly, the way in which he is subsequently ignored by the other prisoners who have raped him is eloquent enough: they have fulfilled their social role as violent enforcers and they have presumably also satisfied their sexual needs, at least until another piece of bait is thrown to them or they find another reason to dump on one of their own. It is also at this time that Tirica stabs Portuga to death, but that is almost an afterthought to the principal event being portrayed, Garoto's rape.

The other limitation of Cury's postrape sequence is a more serious one, and it confirms that the director chooses not to dwell very much on Garoto's handling of what has happened to him. This second limitation takes the form of having Garoto seated, huddled against the bars of the cell, not a very likely position for someone who has been raped by six men. It may be that Cury wishes to pull some punches here for "aesthetic reasons," which is confirmed by the fact that the young man's light-colored pants are not noticeably stained by the violence to which his body has been subjected, as one would expect. Or perhaps Cury wishes to reinforce audience identification by portraying Garoto as less battered than he would realistically be in fact: thus the spectators identify with his psychological pain more than they would if Garoto were to be shown blood-stained from rectal bleeding and contorted by the pain of multiple lacerations. Rape as an act of corrective and instructive violence is meant to tear the body, and the sight of someone who has been gang-raped is hardly seductive. As it is, Garoto's appearance and his display of humiliation are not much more serious than if he were a little boy who'd been given a hard spanking.

Cury's ineptitude/pulling of punches is confirmed when, not very long after, the guards—apparently certain that Garoto has been taken care of as they intended—show up, offhandedly cart Tirica off to another cell so he can be charged with Portuga's murder, and tell Garoto he can leave. As the film ends and the credits begin to roll, Garoto is seen first walking then running down the hall from the cell toward the exit. This ending is very effective—Garoto is escaping from the nightmare of his brief incarceration and is probably more convinced than he was before that it is unwise to come to the attention of the police—but it does not match very well the ambulatory possibilities of someone who has been gang-raped. The intense and accurate depiction of social reality that is the mainstay of Plínio Marcos's theater and its accurate translation into film during the majority of *Barrela* is falsified by a rather trite ending that continues to make Garoto available for facile identification by the film's principally middle-class audience. By retaining the image of Garoto as a "nice" middle-class boy who has fallen into the hands of the corrupt police and into the hell hole of the jail cell populated by violent, murderous prisoners, *Barrela* seems to lose its force as the depiction of a basic social dynamic (the uses of violent rape to enforce social and sexual behavior) and veers off toward an Us/Them mentality: the middle class (the spectator, Garoto) at the hands of a violent underbelly of society (the criminal prisoners, the corrupt police).

Therefore, it is important to focus on a significant plot detail that helps us to hold in mind that Garoto is not just circumstantially a victim, not just someone who has had the misfortune to fall into the hands of the police, but that, as a social subject who has come to the attention of the police, he is being subjected to a calculatedly applied lesson. There is no doubt that Garoto is an entry in a police agenda of social control directed at young men of a certain privileged social class who become rowdy in bars and the like. Although they cannot be charged with much of a crime, they need to be taught a lesson that will make them a little less arrogant and sure of themselves, a little more cautious in exercising a socially symbolic power that exceeds any real power at their disposal: they are, after all, only *filhinhos de papai* and not yet fully endowed machos. Tossing them in for a few hours with hardened criminals will give them a good enough scare so that they will have a bit more respect for social authority in the form of the police. Of course, if in the process they get raped, well, those things happen, especially when your social subjectivity is deficient for the real world in its baldest terms.

The plot detail that must be held onto in order for the spectator to return to an important understanding of how design and bad luck are operating here in the case of Garoto's rape is the fact that Bereco, on this third occasion of the game of Smear the Queer, does not intervene, but is in fact one of the instigators. Indeed, his characterization of Garoto as jailbait is the very first one articulated. Bereco cannot intervene, because it is no longer a question of keeping the other prisoners in order, but of leading them in their fulfillment of their one important function within the economy of the jail, which is to execute the application of corrective rape. Thus, Bereco joins in carrying out that function. That this rape is the primary function of these individuals is made clear by the title of the film. The word *barrela* may have other meanings (ironically, one is the "restoring of a person's good name"), but in jailhouse lingo it means sexual violence. There is a frame to this effect at the beginning of the film just to make sure the spectator is fully aware of what is about to be seen: not just violence, but institutionalized sexual violence.

Cury's *Barrela,* except for the difficulties presented by the detail of the treatment of Garoto's body following his rape, is an excellent adaptation of Marcos's play and, in the process, a fine entry in the inventory of Brazilian filmmaking during the period following the 1964–1985 military dictatorship, particularly as regards the need to provide an adequately theorized interpretation of structural violence.

O beijo no asfalto

Based on Nelson Rodrigues's 1960 play of the same name, Bruno Barreto's *O beijo no asfalto* (1981) captures admirably Rodrigues's fascination with urban life in Rio de Janeiro (cf. Lins, *O teatro de Nelson Rodrigues*), particularly as it relates to sexual issues. Rodrigues's interest in sexual issues concerns principally the intersection between the hegemonic criterion for bourgeois decency, which basically means an endorsement of compulsory

monogamous and reproductive heterosexuality, and the contra-
dictory realities of lived human experience, where such a hegemonic criterion is both difficult to adhere to and, as the source of
both comedy and pathos, essentially impossible to enforce (see
Lockhart, "*Beijo*"; Lockhart, "Nelson Rodrigues"). Rodrigues's
models of the patriarchal enforcers, while at times terrifying, as in
the case of *Beijo,* are also comically pathetic, as in the case of the
father at his wit's end over guarding the virginity of his daughters
in *Os sete gatinhos* (The Seven Kittens, 1958), which was also
made into a movie in 1980 by Nelville d'Almeida.

In the case of *Beijo* the crisis for the patriarchal order stems
from a man who witnesses another man run down by a vehicle on
the street. As the victim lies dying, the protagonist goes over to
him, bends down, and kisses him on the lips. The kiss is witnessed
by other bystanders, noted by reporters who have rushed to the
scene, and captured by a television news crew. The consequences
of his act, which he subsequently insists was a gesture of human
solidarity toward someone dying, are staggering, and the man's
life falls apart. At the end of the film, he too is left dying in the
street, shot down by the father of his wife, an act of blood revenge
that has as much to do with the betrayal of the woman by having
kissed another man in public as it does with also being accused of
seducing his wife's kid sister. If the revelation of a presumed homosexuality is momentous, it is even more monstrous because he
is a married man and a seducer of other women.

Homosexuality, as the domain of same-sex desire, is not the
issue in *Beijo:* it is not even so much at issue as perceived to be at
issue, no matter how baseless this perception turns out to be. Despite the theory everyone seems to hold, there is never any indication that homosexuality is involved, neither in terms of Arangir's
admission of a "real" but until then repressed homoerotic desire
nor in terms of a revelation about a life of same-sex activity hidden
from family and public view. Rather, what makes the event so
monstrous is the fact that Arangir is a married man, and his public
behavior is undeniable, unretractable evidence that he has broken
with the pact of compulsive heterosexuality. While it may be true
that a single same-sex kiss does not confirm the presence of homosexuality, no matter what the motivation behind that kiss, it is

an unacceptable violation of the code of decency and must be dealt with accordingly. Thus, Barreto's film turns basically on a question of social control: sexuality is only a constituent in the structure of social control and its practices of enforcement.

Arangir appears in every respect to be a happily married man. If he goes on to pay attention to his young sister-in-law, that occurs as part of the unleashed chaos that stems from his spontaneous act of charity, since she claims to understand him—it is she who seduces him by being the only one to grasp the selflessness of his public kiss. An alternative reading would insist that she is acting exclusively out of sexual self-interest and only taking advantage of her sister's repudiation of Arangir to claim him for herself. Arangir is otherwise pretty much of a nonentity, an average Carioca petit-bourgeois citizen, who has no idea why all of a sudden the world has come down around his ears. He is suddenly exposed, as much as he would have been had he saved everybody the trouble of speculating about his sexuality and declared from the start that he was now ready to go public about being gay. But of course he does not, since gayness is not what is at issue.

Yet the fact that he denies that there was any erotic motivation for his kiss simply compounds the persecutions to which he is exposed. In the office where Arangir works, Barreto makes full use of the ugly and abundant resources of homophobia, and we see Arangir mocked and harassed by his fellow workers, men and women alike, such that this portion of his world is now intolerable for him. What is especially poignant is that Arangir does not know how to handle himself since he is not a gay man, who—no matter how much in the closet he remains—is nevertheless exposed to those who claim they know infallibly who the queers are and make sure that the queers know they know (even if the objects of their attention are not, in fact, queer). The individual, gay or otherwise, who has life-long experience defending himself against the harassment that comes with being identified, if not confrontationally, at least by rumor, as being gay develops a series of survival strategies. They may include stonewalling, avoidance and evasion, confrontation (usually necessarily violent), and even sexual acquiescence, since the gaybaiter may, in fact, back off in exchange for sexual favors (then, again, he may not, especially if his gay baiting is a front for his own unsatisfied homoerotic desire). I have examined elsewhere how workplace gossip functions as a form of social control, employment advancement, and competitive revenge, in this case precisely as it affects two co-workers in the Argentine film *Otra historia de amor* (Another Love Story, 1986) by América Ortiz de Zárate (see Foster, *Contemporary Argentine Cinema*, 135–149).

But if the individual with an experience of being baited can only hope for a relative accommodation to a routine situation, Arangir, as if he had suddenly decided to declare his gayness openly despite always having been taken for a straight man, has no hope of being able to defend himself against the dramatically changed sexual classification to which his fellow workers submit him, especially because it is not true.

I certainly do not wish to imply that such harassment is appropriate when the victim is gay, nor am I claiming that it would be appropriate if Arangir had overnight decided he was gay. All I mean is that in the first two cases the individual might have some chance of defending himself against homophobic aggression. The fact that Arangir cannot defend himself with truth is what makes him so exposed. Gay baiting, of course, is not about sex. As Eve Kosofsky Sedgwick has shown, the epistemology of the closet essentially functions as a means of social control: because (I think) I know something about you, something that (we all agree) is so particularly horrible that mere knowledge about it is enough to destroy you, perhaps even allow you to be killed, I can exercise an almost absolute control over your behavior. The prison of the closet is not just sexual, but racial, ethnic, or whatever else may be considered a horrible secret and a violation of the social contract. The violation of the social contract that is at issue here is that of compulsory heterosexuality: to deviate from its specification is to fall outside the domain of the decent and, therefore, to fall into the realm of the unprotected, the unlamented, and the victimizable.

Arangir's harassment at the hands of his office mates is repeated when he attempts to return to his home. His wife's humiliation over seeing her husband's sexuality the topic of a television report, a newspaper article, and then neighborhood gossip turns her against him. Arangir is the object of a slur painted on walls near his house saying *veado* (queer, faggot), and he also has a sign with the same word pinned to the back of his clothes by a fellow worker.

Arangir is unable to contend with his wife's anger, in large part because he doesn't even know how to explain himself to her: the man who must exert his homoeroticism at least has some point of departure, some language of being in the world, for explaining himself to his family. Arangir is therefore ripe for seduction by his young sister-in-law, who is the only one who neither ridicules nor humiliates him. It is not clear if she really believes that his kissing of the traffic victim was completely innocent or if her sexual seduction of him is based on the venerable, if disingenuous, belief that a gay man just needs some good sex with a woman to discover that he is not gay anymore (as if sexual acts were all that being gay were about) and whether sincere affection or only her sexual self-interest is involved. That does not really matter, since from Arangir's point of view, to be sexually attracted to his wife's kid sister is completely "natural," since he is a mistakenly persecuted heterosexual.

For some reason, the police feel that they need to get involved. The manifestations of homoerotic identity (i.e., a complex of ways of manifesting in public that one is gay, most notably, cross-dressing) or homoerotic acts do not usually concern Brazilian police unless a public scandal or violence ensues. However, although the uproar over Arangir's kiss does not exactly consist of the sort of scandal the police consider worth investigating, since no one powerful is apparently affected by it, an ambitious police agent decides to make it his business, which of course means that he assumes that the kiss is homoerotic in origin. In his defense, one must observe that, from the point of view of public decency laws, something is indecent if it is perceived by the police to be indecent, at least for purposes of initiating an "investigation." Because the police make use of the preposterous reasoning that those involved are helpless to counter, precisely because it makes no sense, the agent goes after Arangir, who manages to escape out the back window.

Left to face the policeman on her own, Arangir's wife, as his stand-in, herself becomes a victim of police harassment. In the twisted logic of homophobia, just as mothers have traditionally been accused of making their sons gay—principally, it is alleged, by overprotecting them and stunting their assimilation to manly ways (a proposition that blithely ignores the existence of thoroughly acceptably masculine gays)—Arangir's wife, Selminha, is faulted for his gayness by not being enough of a woman to him. The police agent, convinced that she needs to be shown by force what a real man is, demands that she prove to him her female sexuality by obliging her to disrobe. One of the most terrible moments in the movie is his leisurely examination of her genitalia in order to ascertain that she is a functioning woman. The look of pain and humiliation on her face mirrors that of every victim of homophobia as much as it does that of every victim of rape. While the rape of Arangir's wife in conformance with what is conventionally understood by rape would be dramatic enough, her rape by the lecherous gaze of the policeman is especially effective because it makes full use of the close-up visualization allowed by film.

Arangir's final humiliation will come not at the hands of the police, but through the agency of his father-in-law. Fathers-in-law are particularly important agents of the contract of compulsory heterosexuality, since they must ensure that the husband of their daughter fulfills his sexual and social responsibilities as provided for in the marriage bonds. Deviant behavior by the son-in-law demands and legitimates correction by the father-in-law in the overdetermined way in which all publicly identified men to one degree or another enjoy corrective powers over women or those whose relative social power is like that of women, as is the case of children, the elderly, and gays (lesbians are controlled first as women and only secondarily as sexual deviants). In the homophobic narrative, one of the worst things that can happen, in addition to discovering that your son is gay, is to discover that your son-in-law is gay. Gay sons may enjoy some degree of protection by virtue of family affection and blood relation—even though all too often such circumstances heighten the sense of betrayal on the part of the father—but sons-in-law rarely enjoy much protected privilege, and often the slightest hint of scandal or deviance is enough for a father to urge or even demand that his daughter renounce her husband and return to the parental refuge.

Rodrigues's play provides a fascinating bit of rhetorical heightening of the circumstances in which Arangir is gunned down by his father-in-law. As it turns out, the father-in-law is himself a closeted gay, and he has always felt a homoerotic attraction to his son-in-law. He has never acted on this attraction, out of respect for his daughter, but it has meant a degree of affection between the two men that might not always be the case in the lower-middle-class world the two men inhabit. Thus, when the father-in-law thinks he discovers that his son-in-law is gay, while his public execution of Arangir is in reality an act of unrequited love, to society at large it can only be read (since the homophobic narrative would not contemplate any other reading) as an act of blood revenge. This almost absurd (but not nonverisimilar) act of unrequited love provides the ending of Barreto's film with an opening to another level of narrative meaning. That is, instead of closing the story of Arangir's relationship with his wife and, through her, with the codes of compulsory heterosexuality—since he cannot comply with them, it is legitimate that, quite literally, he is taken out of society through an avenging murder—the film suggests a narrative that has up to that point not been broached: the homosexual who comes out of the closet is not Arangir with his public kiss, but his father-in-law with his public assassination. Given the degree to which the homophobic narrative cannot accept same-sex love to begin with, the possibility of a father-in-law being in love with his son-in-law is tantamount to ridiculous. What Barreto does is leave the spectator with the demand to contemplate a whole new set of relationships, which alter the stable family unit one thought had only been altered for the first time by Arangir's public kiss. In reality, patriarchal stability had always existed in a precarious way by virtue of a closeted homoerotic attraction.

Thus, Barreto's film places two requirements on the spectators. In the first place, it requires that they contemplate in detail the disastrous effects of homophobic discourse, as it begins in the murmurs surrounding Arangir's planting of the kiss on the traffic victim's mouth, as it continues with the interpretations of the broadcast media, as it takes a deeply ugly turn with the harassment Arangir receives in the workplace and his wife receives at the hands of the police, and finally as it climaxes in the apparent exercise of patriarchal justice. At the same time as spectators are required to contemplate homophobia—and, regrettably, few can be counted on to be free of it, since it is one of the many zero degree components of our social reality—they are also asked to contemplate a homoerotic narrative that goes beyond what most spectators have been familiar with. Although homophobia is ready to acknowledge any form of pairing, in a crescendo of degenerate couplings whereby each instance proves the vileness of each and every one of them, the nuclear narrative it circulates is that of a feminine/feminized man who assumes the female gender role with a masculine man. This dominant scheme, whereby one man substitutes for a woman in the heterosexual paradigm, leaves little room for any other combinations, such as two "feminine" men or two "masculine" men. Complicating these alternatives with cross-generational combinations, such as father-in-law and son-in-law, is too much for the run-of-the-mill homophobic plot. By closing his film with precisely such a major plot innovation, Barreto runs the risk of rejection by spectators outraged over what might be supposed to be a flagrant proposition. Or, as a more favorable alternative, Barreto leaves his spectators no longer wondering about why Arangir kissed the dying man—this has long ceased to be of any importance—and contemplating a major narrative defiance of the homophobic plot: an erotic triangle that may lead them to contemplate, perhaps to question, the bases on which homophobia is constructed.

However, the film cannot escape an ideological trap. No matter how much it may wish to provoke in spectators the basis for the construction of homosexuality and the tyranny of homophobia, the plot works as though to say, "See, Arangir is okay after all, because he is not gay; the one who is gay is his father-in-law." Thus, gayness as a negative social marker is deftly and suddenly shifted in a definitive manner from Arangir and placed on the shoulders of someone else, who, as a murderer, remains negatively marked. Since the homophobic mind often associates mental instability and criminality with the homosexual, the shooting confirms a powerful stereotype. And since there is no opportunity, with the quick closure of the film, to explore how violence, even murderous violence, is the consequence of the violence of the closet within which homophobia confines the father-in-law, the spectators are still left with very much of an opportunity to leave the theater thinking that violence is, after all, the birthright of the homosexual.

The only difference is that it is no longer the violence of homophobia against the reputedly gay man, but the violence generated by the actual gay man. The closing scene of the film, as Selminha's father cradles the dead or dying body of his son-in-law, is grotesquely ironic. The scene is held for the time it takes the credits to role, and it is a same-sex restaging of the Pietà. But the allusion is no longer to the socially overdetermined love of mother for sacrificed son, but to the homophobic victim of the patriarchal father. It may be his father-in-law, but the law, in the enforcement of sexuality, knows no distinction. It would be reasonable to suppose that the murderer, who can claim as much that he was protecting the honor of one daughter as that of the other, will never be prosecuted for the way in which he has settled accounts in the name of both of his daughters and their social roles as much as he has avenged the way in which Arangir never responded to the other man's love—indeed, most certainly never even knew it existed.

Both of the films examined so far provided complex interpretations of homophobia, and both significantly occur in the context of police/state power. Indeed, it is obvious that both authors and their cinematographic interpreters see homophobia as an instrument of social control exercised with unchallenged power by the police and criminal justice system, an interpretation that is also present in Héctor Babenco's 1985 Brazilian-American film in English, *Kiss of the Spider Woman,* based on Manuel Puig's 1976 novel of the same name.

Homophobia makes use of a sexuality of no specifically homoerotic content in *Barrela,* which might be called a queer text because of its examination of nonstraight uses of sex, but it certainly cannot be called a gay one. Indeed, it is questionable whether Marcos, in his extensive dramaturgy that makes use of homosexual motifs, can ever be said really to move from the homosexual as a dimension of dirty realism to anything approaching homoeroticism as a matter of legitimate social rights.

Rodrigues and director Barreto of the film version can see things in a much different light. While there is certainly homophobia on the part of the police apparatus and the general social text from which it derives its highly rhetoricized discourse of social control, and while there is also homophobia manifested in the case of specific individuals whose horizons of knowledge are confined and defined by that discourse, *O beijo no asfalto,* because of Rodrigues's remarkably subtle analysis of human nature that runs throughout all of his dramaturgy, uncovers homoerotic feeling beneath the ugly incrustations of homophobic hatred. Indeed, the Pietà image with which the film concludes is a strikingly affirmative discovery within the dreadfulness of Arangir's experience and the profoundly pathetic, perhaps even tragic, sexual repression of his father-in-law, who can only love Arangir's body after he has killed him. Within the realm of a necrophilia that is an objective correlative of homophobia, *Beijo* does, nevertheless, end with an expression of tender love. Rodrigues's irony is truly dramatic here, and Barreto does well to respect it. The result is certainly the first Brazilian film that undertakes anything approximating a serious analysis of the confrontation between homophobia and homoerotic desire, and it is significant that it was made during the military dictatorship, a full five years before the return to constitutional democracy and the redemocratization of Brazilian culture.

Vera

Sérgio Toledo's 1987 film about an orphan who desperately wants a sex change operation to replace the female body with which she has been cursed, in order to be a real man, might just as well have been discussed under the heading of crises in masculinity rather than under the rubric of gender trouble. Nevertheless, Toledo's character is complex enough and his ending is open enough that Vera, who prefers to call herself Paulo, is shown as torn equally between insisting on being a man and accepting the demands of her sometime lover, Clara, that they love each other as women. At the end of the film, after a desperate flight from Clara, who insists on undressing Vera/Paulo so that they may love as two female bodies, Vera is shown confessing to herself that there is only one thing left for her to do. However, it is left for the spectator to decide if that one thing is suicide (there is at least one false alarm in this regard), a continued insistence on following through with her desire to reconfigure her body as a man (the film opens and closes with U.S. space probe images, and the phallic images echo Vera's assertion that she can find in America the science to assist her quest for maleness), or acceptance of Clara's proposal that they love as women. The fact that Toledo's film is titled *Vera* rather than *Paulo* would seem to indicate that he prefers to hold this social subject within the realm of female identity. Yet there are good reasons given for Vera to want a change of sexual and gender venue.

Raised in an orphanage that has all of the trappings of combined mental hospital and juvenile reformatory—inmates are routinely restrained as though they were committed and punished by serving terms—Vera sees the miserably dependent, marginal, and humiliating lot of women. The institution is a masculine establishment, and Vera and her colleagues are routinely harangued by a warden who is more concerned with their nonfemininity than he is with reports that they are being sexually abused by the guards: at one point, Vera is put into solitary confinement to "think" about the error of having raised the issue. The inmates are organized into families for self-protection, with older girls who assume masculine postures serving as their "fathers." As one inmate claims, the latter are not really lesbians, since the majority of them, upon leaving the institution when they become of age, pursue conventional female lives on the outside. The warden attempts to feminize his charges by organizing a dance with boys from the male wing of the orphanage, but the girls see the introduction of forced contact with men as disrupting their internal solidarity. In angry desperation, the warden attempts to force the girls to get rid of their "masculine" apparel (jeans and flannel shirts) and to dress as women. When they balk, he orders them to drop their pants: if they want to act like men, they have to prove they have the balls that confirm their maleness.

As in Héctor Babenco's *Pixote* (1981), the orphanage is a microcosm of society at large, and learning how to survive there is harsh education required to make it on the outside. It is in the institutional context of the humiliation of femaleness that Vera comes to the conclusion that she must redefine herself as a man. With the aid of a male psychologist, whose name appears to be the inspiration for the name "Paulo" that Vera insists on being called, she is given a job in the library of the research institute where he works. Although the psychologist's family and the female employees are uncomfortable with Vera's masculine traits, they can accept even less her appearance at work one morning correctly dressed as a man, in a suit and tie; the psychologist is able to protect Vera's job by having her reassigned within the institute.

The main narrative conflict of the film involves Vera's relationship with Clara. When Vera publishes a poem in a literary journal of the institute and dedicates it to Clara, the latter is angry at what she sees as a betrayal of their friendship and the public insinuation of a dangerous relationship. Vera shows up at Clara's house dressed as a man and wins the confidence of Clara's parents and the adoration of her little boy, whom she is raising alone; a serious relationship ensues. Clara at one point asks Vera how she was able to deceive her parents, and Vera replies that no deceit was intended: they simply came to their own conclusions, based, one would add, on their reading of conventional signs that Vera's gender enactment puts into play. At first alarmed by what she sees as Vera's charade, Clara falls in love with her—if I continue at this point to insist on calling Toledo's protagonist Vera, rather than Paulo, it is not because Toledo does, but because it is Clara who insists on viewing her lover as a woman.

There is a telling erotic scene in which the two begin to make love. Clara is naked, and the signs of her female body are explicitly evident. Vera is only partially undressed, and when Clara attempts to remove the rest of her clothes so that the love scene they have begun can continue unfettered, Vera stops her, saying that she will never remove her clothes. At the end of the film, in another erotic moment, Clara provokes Vera's flight by succeeding in removing the binding that flattens Vera's breasts, and it is only here that for the first time the spectator sees these crucial secondary sex signs that would confirm Vera's body as female. But Vera, sensing she has lost control of the relationship, bolts, and we see her grabbing her male clothes from Clara. She is dressed in these clothes in the final sequences as she sits on the grounds of the institute in solitary reflection, seeks out the psychologist, and then confronts her final, if ambiguous, decision in the film's conclusion.

Vested Interests: Cross-Dressing and Cultural Anxiety is the title of Marjorie B. Garber's study of clothing as, one might say, a complex of tertiary sexual signs, such that transgression in the utilization of conventional gender-grounded dressing is often considered a renunciation of a biologically assigned sexual identity. Dress as gender enactment and sexual identity as biological destiny are homologized by societal convention because of the perceived need to maintain a criterion of binary heterosexuality. It is for this reason that the warden of the orphanage is outraged by the nonfemininity of the dress of the girls under his charge, which he also equates with the lesbianism that exists among them (pants and testicles must necessarily go together and confirm each other mutually), and it is also for this reason that employees of the institute are appalled when Vera shows up in male attire. When one of the severely matriarchal employees tells her that she cannot come to work dressed "that way," Vera asserts that her dress is a model of correctness and points to a male employee less correctly dressed than she is because he is not wearing a tie.

Toledo's film in this fashion skillfully negotiates questions of hegemonic sexual identity, in which for a woman to cross-dress as a man is an outrageous invasion of the domain of male superiority, while for a man to cross-dress as a woman is a shameful assumption of an inferior social status. It seems that Vera's principal attraction to masculinity is the social power that comes with it in a society in which we see her repeatedly witnessing the degradation of women. The famous formulation by Judith Butler in the title of her book *Gender Trouble* is to be understood not as a deviation from a presumed gender norm, but as a questioning of so-called naturalized sexual roles. In one sense, this is what is going on in *Vera*, as part of her nonconformity with being a woman in a society in which the power for survival accrues only to males; as the "father" of one of the "families" in the orphanage tells Vera, "you are nothing unless you have a father to protect you." In this way, Vera's attitude is one of total repudiation of her biological destiny as a woman, and her assimilation to masculinity is so determined that, at one point, Clara complains that she is acting "just like a man" when she expresses her jealousy over seeing Clara speaking intimately with a male co-worker.

Toledo's film would be interesting enough if it were an allegory of female humiliation and the quest for masculine identity on the part of a woman as a means of evading that humiliation and acceding to male power. The film crosses that interpretive issue with the question of a lesbian love relationship between Vera and Clara. While Clara is uneasy at first with Vera's interest in her, she eventually is even more uneasy with Vera's inability to respond sexually as a woman and her insistence on maintaining, even in private, her self-construction as a man, even at the expense of disrupting the erotic program that develops between the two of them. It is interesting to speculate on which of these two possibilities is the most problematical for the spectator, Vera as transgendered or Vera as a lesbian lover, or whether it is an exponentially more problematical compound of the two.

There is a telling scene toward the end of the film, when Vera has fled from Clara's insistence that she respond to her as a woman: indeed, Clara insists on calling Vera by the feminine form of the name she prefers—Paula. Vera seeks the assistance of the psychologist who has befriended her. She asks to use the bathroom, saying that she does not feel well. When she doesn't come back, the look of concern on the psychologist's face indicates that something is wrong, with the clear implication that she has locked herself in the bathroom to commit suicide. When she finally responds to the psychologist's insistence that she open the door, we see her sitting on the toilet with her hands between her legs. She withdraws her hands and extends them toward the psychologist and the camera: they are covered in blood, presumably because she is menstruating. This segment serves to confirm Toledo's greater interest in continuing to see Vera, despite her own protestations, as a woman.

Such an insistence on the male director's part is not without problems, despite how some spectators may wish to sort the film out in terms of a confirmation of the validity of a lesbian sexual relationship between Vera and Clara. Toledo insists on crossing the lesbian subtext with a larger issue of gender identity in which the validity of Vera's sex-change project is questioned by the very fact of maintaining her female name as the film's title. This could well be seen as a masculinist exception to what the woman herself sees as a legitimate aspiration, and, indeed, Toledo would appear to support that aspiration in large measure, since his film reinforces Vera's perception that there is little social or symbolic advantage in being a woman. The fact that the ending of the film is ambiguous as to what Vera will do seems to suggest that Toledo himself is unsure of what her fate might be. In any event, it is interesting to note that alternate sexual rights have frequently been cast in recent years in terms of the need to recognize the legitimacy of cross-gendering (especially in Argentina, where it is a very public discussion and one of the bases for the reformulation of police codes affecting public decency).

But such a discussion has been cast exclusively in terms of men wishing to identify themselves as women, including reconstructive surgery. As far as I know, Toledo's film is a unique cultural product in its dealing with a woman whose goal is not only to identify herself as a man, but to seek reconstructive surgery to this effect. When the psychologist who befriends her questions such a possibility, Vera affirms her belief that she will be able to carry out her plans in America. The fact that Toledo does not tell the audience what Vera means by her final statement that she knows what she is going to have to do suggests that sexual politics in Brazil remain confusing enough for it to be impossible to sort Vera's case out. In any event, the issues that *Vera* raises, in terms of sexual oppression, gender trouble, and lesbian desire, make it indeed quite an exceptional first film.

There is less to be said about commonalities among the three films examined in this section, except to express the wish that there were more texts to deal with. Given the growing imperative for homoerotic visibility in Latin American capitals, there can be little doubt, unless a reactionary movement imposes itself, that in coming decades cinematographic visibility will match the visibility already attained in literature and other cultural genres. If filmmaking on lesbigay themes lags behind, it is because of the in-your-face visibility provided by film images, by the fact that films have a more public distribution than does literature, and by what can be a very discomforting experience in that films are customarily viewed with other people, whether in the movie theater or in a domestic setting. As such, the spectator's response, including acute embarrassment or disgust, is potentially a shared reaction, which may only serve to compound it exponentially. Nevertheless, the growing treatment of gays in less homophobic terms in the press and on television (which also often involves shared spectatorship) augurs well for increased filmic interpretations.

Barrela certainly exemplifies an abiding homophobia without any opening toward a legitimation of same-sex desire. Homosexual acts, while they involve some degree of pleasure for the so-called active participant, are shown to be more part of a power struggle than anything else and, specifically in terms of the police's deliverance of a young middle-class man up to his inevitable rape by prison oldtimers, to be a technique of social control.

Homophobia and rape are also integral to O *beijo no asfalto*, and it could also be argued that the representation of homoerotic desire does not figure prominently. But of course it does, in at least in two ways. First of all, once we have taken into account Arangir's assertion that the kiss he gave to the dying man was not homoerotic and once we have, with considerable difficulty and application, peeled away the thick crust of homophobia that adheres to him because of that kiss, there may remain the feeling of "Why not?" Why couldn't Arangir's kiss have had a dimension of homoerotic intensity, as the motivation, as the experience, or as the recollection of it? Certainly, the violence to which he is subject must necessarily distract him from any consideration of desire on one or more of these levels, but the simple fact is that homophobia has not, to date, been capable of destroying homoerotic desire. It can only destroy that desire by destroying the individuals who experience it.

In the second place, there is homoerotic desire represented in the film, if only materially in the long closing simulacrum of the Pietà. Arangir's father-in-law is the final instrument of homophobic violence, which he turns against himself by killing the object of his own long-lived homoerotic passion. The film has no room to explore that passion or even to legitimate it, except in the ways in which it is merciless in its portrayal of homophobic violence and in the melodramatic effects of the Pietà sequence, which obliges the audience to contemplate this long, if futile, embrace (one wonders if Barreto considered having the father-in-law kiss the body of the object of his desire, but rejected this possibility as excessively melodramatic).

Vera, then, becomes the only film that is a sustained examination of what can be called the issues on a lesbigay or queer agenda.[4] By exploring the question of gender transgression and by showing that such transgressions cannot be easily carried out or assimilated by any of the individuals involved, Toledo's film eschews a facile approach to sexual desire that belies movement slogans and shows how much sociocultural work remains to be done in this area of human rights.

Conclusions

The vitality of contemporary Brazilian filmmaking can easily be demonstrated by reference to the numbers of films that are produced every year in Brazil and the ambitious efforts that have taken place since the return to constitutional democracy in 1985. The fact that Brazilian films have been candidates for the Oscar awarded to the best foreign film for two years running may indicate the eagerness with which the industry has done what is necessary to compete internationally. But it also indicates honest attempts to deal with events in Brazilian history that are of international interest. Moreover, the emergence of a respectable core of women filmmakers is also of cultural significance. Yet the degree to which same-sex relations remain hidden, except for only a few cases, and the effort that must be made to read through the facade of compulsory heterosexuality to assay issues of homosocialism that shade off into homoeroticism are a less than encouraging aspect of the films made since 1985, especially when one views the films of homoerotic desire and sexual difference that have been made in the same period in Mexico, Argentina, Spain, and even Cuba.

My choice of gender relations as the organizing principle of this book is based neither on the premise that such relations are unique to post-1985 filmmaking (gender is the ground zero of virtually all filmmaking) nor on the premise that the films examined have anything uniquely Brazilian to say about gender, even though some paradigmatic Brazilian images, if not tired stereotypes, regarding gender do emerge in films like *Bananas Is My Business* (the Latin bombshell), *Jorge um brasileiro* (the Brazilian super-man), and *Ópera do malandro* (the gangster as a highly sexualized subject, by contrast to the almost asexual American gangster à la James Cagney or Edward G. Robinson). Rather, it is chiefly the consequence of my own personal commitment, through my estab-lished research agenda, to dealing with gender issues, especially those involving so-called gender trouble. This brings with it the imperative to examine gender constructions in terms of themes and dimensions that remain buried under the conventionality of gen-der interpretations that are the not very surprising result of the conventionality of those gender constructions: the naturalization of gender constructions also naturalizes the bases of our interpre-tation of them, without the intellectual work required by the criti-cal enterprise.

Undoubtedly there are films I have overlooked, and others will correct this record through reviews and their own original scholarship: I hope it is most corrected, however, by the cine-matographic production that will come out of Brazil in the next decade or so. Since I have claimed from the outset that this is not a comprehensive guide to post-1985 filmmaking, I am less con-cerned about what films I may have overlooked than I am about the ways in which I have written about those films I have exam-ined. Concomitantly, I am less concerned with those who may dis-miss gender-grounded criticism, inspired by feminist and queer theories, as irrelevant than I am about the abiding ethical ques-tions about how a foreign scholar examines a cultural production which is not "native" to him (the quotation marks refer to the need not to leave this ideologically charged term unexamined). This ethical concern has little to do with any regret in applying what may be denounced as alien theories (this is also a separate ideologically charged debate). Rather, it has everything to do with the sheer pleasure the critic can derive, as Zavarzadeh says, from seeing films politically, knowing that they have deep and contra-dictory meanings and that the elaboration of a coherent metatext about those meanings is fraught with many perils, not the least of which is simply to have been blindsided by the text. Having worked in both literature and film, I consider film a much more problematical critical enterprise precisely because the image tends to trick the viewer, even the viewer who is an experienced critic, into believing that what is being seen is unmediated reality, something less likely to happen with the artificiality of letters, in literature. Yet, of course, the gender constructions that appear in these films, no matter what the consciously contestatorial nature of the filmmakers may have been, are not unmediated, as, to be sure, my own readings are not unmediated. So, in the final analysis, I wish to underscore the mediated nature of my own interpretations, as a foreign scholar, as a feminist and queer scholar, as a scholar whose discourse is underlain by a complex and not always altogether felicitous conjunction of theoretical principles, and as, simply, a selective participant in the enterprise of Brazilian filmmaking.

Notes

INTRODUCTION

1. A figure that, in turn, goes back to the Lusitanian giant as found in the figure of Adamastor in Luís Vaz de Camões's late Renaissance epic, *Os lusíadas* (1572), which describes Vasco da Gama's discovery of a sea route to India.

1. CONSTRUCTIONS OF MASCULINITY

1. It is important to note that Barreto's film diverges significantly from the novel by Domingos Olympio, published sometime in the 1880s (exact date unknown). In Olympio's novel, Luzia is represented as much more masculine than in Barreto's film. She is killed fighting a man who attempts to kill her best friend, a prostitute named Terezinha. It should also be mentioned that the crossgendering that is central to *Luzia homem* also evokes João Guimarães Rosa's *Grande sertão: veredas* (1956). The crossgendering motif in Rosa's novel and its homosexual dimensions are discussed by Roberto Reis, "João Guimarães Rosa," in *Latin American Writers on Gay and Lesbian Themes: A Bio-Critical Sourcebook*.

2. The political polemicist Noam Chomsky, in an interview with Marilyn A. Zeitlin, observes that "Brazil is an interesting case because the US took it over in 1945 and was going to turn it into what they called a testing ground, for scientific methods of economic development. And it was virtually run by US technocrats who followed all the rules, all the neo-liberal rules, and it was considered a tremendous economic success, as indeed it was for about 5 or 10 percent of the popu-

lation. For about 80 or 85, it was sort of like central Africa" ("El Salvador and Global Colonialism," 98).

3.
JOÃO ALEGRE [= Otto in the film]
   Telegram
   From Alabama
   For Mr. Max
   Overseas
   Ah, good God in heaven
   I feel so happy
TERESINHA [= Ludmila in the film]
   The confirmation arrived
   From United such and such
   That they are giving us the franchise
   For tropical nylon
MAX
   So then we'll put in
   A factory in São Paulo
TERESINHA
   And then we're going to export
   Nylon thread to Japan
MAX
   I know nylon is worth a lot
   But I'm starting to get tired of it
   I had really a better idea
   We're going to diversify
TERESINHA
   I've already diversified, hah hah
   I made a deal with Shell
   Coca-Cola, RCA
   And it's going to be real great
CORO
   Fabulous
   The money's
   Rolling in
   From the home base
   Ah, good God in heaven
   I feel so happy. (182)

4. In 1982 Back released *República guarani* (Guarani Republic). Although in it he explores the ambiguities surrounding whether or not

the Jesuit missions in Paraguay during the colonial period had as their goal the establishment of a Jesuit empire, it is much more of a conventional documentary than is his work in the late 1980s and 1990s as exemplified by *Yndio do Brasil*.

5.
Indian of America,
we preached our gospel
for your bitter suicide
we preached our gospel
for your suicide that cost so much.

6.
a father without country
a country without father.

2. CONSTRUCTIONS OF FEMININE AND FEMINIST IDENTITIES

1. Any consideration of Pagu's fate is enough to make one sick. How could a person so full of life with so much to give be crushed down to the point of taking her own life? Does it have to do with her being a woman? Is it a question of politics? Does it have to do with the period in which she lived?

2. Pagu is, of course, part of a nascent feminist movement in Brazil, which includes other activists such as Maria Lacerda de Moura, Lutz, and Ercília Nogueira Cobra, to mention only the most well known.

3. For a more conventional documentary, see Tetê Moraes's 1987 *Terra para Rose* (Land for Rose), which focuses on one woman's participation in the invasion by approximately eight thousand peasants in 1985 of land belonging to the Fazenda Anoni in Rio Grande do Sul. Occurring at the time of the transition from military dictatorship to democracy, the march, the invasion, and the occupation represented a challenge between, on the one hand, a return to citizens' rights and, on the other, the rights of property that the military had defended. The military triumphs, and Rose is killed in the ensuing efforts of Anoni to reclaim his land with the assistance of the military. The documentary, however, is open-ended, in the sense that it looks toward the return to democracy as the possible vindication of the rights of landless peasants. In terms of a feminist dimension, by focusing on Rose, the documen-

tary underscores the role of women in maintaining familial, and therefore personal, identity in the face of the circumstances of anonymous
landlessness and the tremendous dislocations associated with popular
struggle. In this sense, one of the key scenes in the film is the image of
Rose speaking about peasant rights and the legitimacy of the invasion
while at the same time nursing her child.

4. Roberts also notes that Miranda was always a popular favorite
among the female impersonators in the U.S. armed forces entertainment troops, including the fact that "the gay servicemen who turned
Miranda into an immediate camp icon recognized her parody of gender
roles and were able to use her text in impersonations at camp shows as
an allowable expression of their subjectivity" ("The Lady in the Tutti-
Frutti Hat," 19). Furthermore, Bérubé, writing on gays in the U.S.
armed forces during World War II, notes: "The female character most
impersonated by GIs, whether they were gay or not, was also the
campiest movie star of the early 1940s—Carmen Miranda. . . . The
Carmen Miranda drag routine was so common in GI shows that it became a tired cliché and the subject of parody. . . . Gay GIs who did
Carmen Miranda could easily slip a gay sensibility into their acts"
(*Coming Out under Fire,* 89). From what Bérubé says, if Miranda was
extensively parodied, the parodies themselves came to be parodied.

3. SAME-SEX POSITIONINGS AND SOCIAL POWER

1. Not of my daughter. I was jealous of you. Yes, I am! Ever since
the two of you fell in love, I never say your name. I swore to myself I
would only say your name over your dead body. I want you to die
knowing that. My hatred is love.

2.

Bereco. Daddy's little boy.

Portuga. Looks just like a little girl.

Bahia. Pretty boy.

Tirica. I want to see who's the macho now.

Fumaça. What's going on? You think you're going to jump the boy now?

Tirica. Isn't it bad times for all of us? We're going to cornhole him.

Louco. Give it to him, give it to him up the ass!

3. In Arnaldo Jabor's 1973 film *Toda nudez será castigada* (All
Nudity Will Be Punished), based on a play by Nelson Rodrigues, a *fil-
hino de papai* is also sent to prison and gang-raped. However, in the

last scenes of the film, as the father's wife is dying from slashing her wrists, the young man is seen running away with one of the men who raped him in prison.

4. Walter Hugo Khouri's highly controversial film *Note vazia* (Empty Night, 1964), starring Norma Bengell (who has been mentioned previously with reference to *Os cafajestes*), is noteworthy for its Neorealist representation of bored playboys who decide to insist on a sexual encounter between their dates. Such a representation, however, cannot be claimed to be lesbian in any significant sense, since it takes place within the context of masculine sexual needs, rather than as a woman-motivated resistance to them: sex between women, observed by men, is only a prelude to the "real" thing, whereby the woman exchanges an unsatisfactory same-sex partner for a man who is able to provide her with a satisfactory climax (see Benson, "Between Women").

References

FILMOGRAPHY

Bananas Is My Business. Dir. Helena Solberg and David Meyer. Script: Helena Solberg. International Cinema, Fox Lerner, 1994.

Barrela (escola de crimes). Dir. Marco Antonio Cury. Script: Plínio Marcos. Sagres Cinema Televisão Video, 1990.

O beijo no asfalto. Dir. Bruno Barreto. Script: Doc Comparato. Sistema Globo de Comunicação, 1981.

O boto. Dir. Walter Lima Júnior. Script: Walter Lima Júnior. Fox Lorber, 1987.

Capitalismo selvagem. Dir. André Klotzel. Script: André Klotzel and Ojalma Limongi Batista. Sagres Cinema Televisão Video, 1993.

Eternamente Pagu. Dir. Norma Bengell. Script: Márcia de Almeida, Geraldo Carneiro, and Norma Bengell. Sistema Globo de Comunicação, 1987.

A hora da estrela. Dir. Suzana Amaral. Script: Suzana Amaral and Alfredo Oróz. Story: Clarice Lispector. Raiz Produções Cinematográficas, 1985.

Jorge o brasileiro. Dir. Paulo Thiago. Script: Paulo Thiago. Trans Video, Embrafilm. Encontro Produções Cinematográficas, 1989.

Lamarca. Dir. Sérgio Rezende. Script: Sérgio Rezende and Alfredo Oróz. Sagres Cinema Televisão Video, 1994.

Ópera do malandro. Dir. Rui Guerra. Script: Chico Buarque, Orlando Senna, and Rui Guerra. Sistema Globo de Comunicação, Embrafilm, 1986.

Que bom te ver viva. Dir. Lúcia Murat. Script: Lúcia Murat. Fundação do Cinema Brasileiro, 1989.

Vera. Dir. Sérgio Toledo. Script: Sérgio Toledo. Richard Leacok Produções, 1987.

Yndio do Brasil. Dir. Sylvio Back. Script: Sylvio Back. Este Film, 1995.

CRITICISM

Albuquerque, Severino João. *Violent Acts: A Study of Contemporary Latin American Theatre.* Detroit: Wayne State University Press, 1991.

Allodi, Federico A. "Women as Torture Victims." *Canadian Journal of Psychiatry* 35, no. 2 (1990): 144–148.

Araujo, Denize Correa. "The Spheres of Power in *Xica da Silva.*" *Rocky Mountain Review* 46, nos. 1–2 (1992): 37–43.

Back, Sylvio. *Yndio do Brasil: Poemas do filme.* N.p.: Gráfico Ouro Preto, 1995.

Bell-Metereau, Rebecca. *Hollywood and Androgyny.* 2nd ed. New York: Columbia University Press, 1993.

Benson, Pater. "Between Women: Lesbianism in Pornography." *Textual Practice* 7, no. 3 (1993): 412–427.

Bérubé, Allan. *Coming Out under Fire: The History of Gay Men and Women in World War Two.* New York: Penguin, 1991. Orig. New York: Free Press, 1990.

Bloch, Jayne H. "Patrícia Galvão: The Struggle against Conformity." *Latin American Literary Review* 27 (1986): 188–201.

Borim, Dário, Jr. "Fernando Paulo Nagle Gabeira." In *Latin American Writers on Gay and Lesbian Themes: A Bio-Critical Sourcebook,* ed. David William Foster, 160–166.

Brasil: Nunca mais. Petrópolis: Vozes, 1985. English trans.: Catholic Church, Archdiocese of São Paulo. *Torture in Brazil.* Trans. Jaime Wright. Ed. Joan Dassin. New York: Vintage Books, 1986.

Brazilian Cinema. Expanded edition. Ed. Randal Johnson and Robert Stam. New York: Columbia University Press, 1995. Orig. 1982.

Bueno, Eva Paulino. "Adolfo Caminha." In *Latin American Writers on Gay and Lesbian Themes: A Bio-Critical Sourcebook,* ed. David William Foster, 94–100.

Bunster, Ximena. "The Torture of Women Political Prisoners: A Case Study in Female Sexual Slavery." In Global Feminist Workshop to Organize against Traffic in Women, *International Feminism: Networking against Female Sexual Slavery,* ed. Kathleen Barry et al., 94–102. New York: Women's Tribune Centre, 1984.

Burton, Julianne. *The Social Documentary in Latin America*. Pittsburgh: University of Pittsburgh Press, 1990.

Butler, Judith. *Gender Trouble: Feminism and the Subversion of Identity*. New York: Routledge, 1990.

Camargo, Robson Corrêa de. "Un diálogo constante y fructífero." *Teatro al sur: Revista latinoamericana* 2, no. 3 (1995): 20–24.

Campos, Augusto de. *Pagu: Patrícia Galvão, vida-obra*. Rio de Janeiro: Brasiliense, 1982.

Cardoso, Abel, Júnior. *Carmen Miranda, a cantora do Brasil*. São Paulo: n.p., 1978.

Cinema and Social Change in Latin America: Conversations with Filmmakers. Ed. Julianne Burton. Austin: University of Texas Press, 1986.

Daly, Mary. *Pure Lust: Elemental Feminist Philosophy*. Boston: Beacon Press, 1984.

Davis, Darién J. Review of *Bananas Is My Business*. *American Historical Review* 101, no. 4 (1996): 1162–1164.

de Lauretis, Teresa. *Technologies of Gender: Essays on Theory, Film, and Fiction*. Bloomington: Indiana University Press, 1987.

Dollimore, Jonathan. *Sexual Dissidence: Augustine to Wilde, Freud to Foucault*. Oxford: Clarendon Press, 1991.

Doty, Alexander. *Making Things Perfectly Queer: Interpreting Mass Culture*. Minneapolis: University of Minnesota Press, 1993.

Duarte, Eduardo de Assis. "Eficácia e limites do discurso ideológico em *Parque industrial*, de Patrícia Galvão." *Suplemento literário, Minas Gerais* 1105 (September 3, 1988): 6–7.

Dulles, John W. F. *Brazilian Communism, 1935–1945: Repression during World Upheaval*. Austin: University of Texas Press, 1983.

Dworkin, Andrea. *Intercourse*. New York: Free Press, 1987.

Dyer, Alexander. "There's Something Queer Here." In *Out in Culture: Gay, Lesbian, and Queer Essays on Popular Culture*, ed. Corey K. Creekmur and Alexander Doty, 71–90. Durham: Duke University Press, 1995.

Foster, David William. *Contemporary Argentine Cinema*. Columbia: University of Missouri Press, 1992.

———. "Do 'para inglês ver' ao 'para brasileiro entender': escrevendo o socio-texto homo-erótico brasileiro." *Mester* 24, no. 1 (Spring 1995): 63–73.

———. "Glauco Mattoso." In *Latin American Writers on Gay and Lesbian Themes: A Bio-Critical Sourcebook*, ed. David William Foster, 217–220.

————. "Latin American Documentary Narrative." *PMLA: Publications of the Modern Language Association of America* 99 (1984): 41–55.

————, ed. *Latin American Writers on Gay and Lesbian Themes: A Bio-Critical Sourcebook.* Westport, Conn.: Greenwood Press, 1995.

França, Oswaldo. *Jorge, um brasileiro.* 13th ed. Rio de Janeiro: Nova Fronteira, 1989. Orig. 1967.

Fuchs, Cynthia J. "The Buddy Politic." In *Screening the Male: Exploring Masculinities in Hollywood Cinema,* ed. Steven Cohan and Ina Rae Hark, 194–210. London: Routledge, 1993.

Galvão, Patrícia. *Parque industrial.* Prefácio de Geraldo Ferraz; apresentação de Flávio Loureiro Chaves. 3rd ed. Porto Alegre: Mercado Aberto; São Paulo: EDUFSCar, 1994. Orig. 1933. Trans. as *Industrial Park: A Proletarian Novel.* Trans. and foreword by Elizabeth Jackson and K. David Jackson. Lincoln: University of Nebraska Press, 1993.

Garber, Marjorie B. *Vested Interests: Cross-Dressing and Cultural Anxiety.* New York: Routledge, 1992.

George, David. *The Modern Brazilian Stage.* Austin: University of Texas Press, 1992.

Gil-Montero, Martha. *Brazilian Bombshell: The Biography of Carmen Miranda.* New York: Donald I. Fine, 1989.

Graziano, Frank. *Divine Violence: Spectacle, Psychosexuality and Radical Christianity in the Argentine "Dirty War."* Boulder: Westview Press, 1992.

Guevara, Ernesto. *El diario del Che en Bolivia.* Prólogo de Fidel Castro. Mexico City: Siglo XXI, 1968. Numerous subsequent editions.

Hoin. Review of *Barrela. Variety* 339, no. 4 (April 25, 1990): 34.

Hollanda, Chico Buarque de. *Ópera do malandro: Comédia musical.* 2nd ed. São Paulo: Livraria Cultura Editora, 1979. Orig. 1978.

Irigaray, Luce. *Ce Sexe qui n'est pas un.* Paris: Éditions de Minuit, 1977. Trans. as *This Sex Which Is Not One.* Trans. Catherine Porter with Carolyn Burke. Ithaca: Cornell University Press, 1985.

Jackson, K. David. "Afterword." In Patrícia Galvão, *Industrial Park,* trans. Elizabeth Jackson and K. David Jackson, 115–153. Lincoln: University of Nebraska Press, 1993.

————. "Alienation and Ideology in *A famosa revista* (1945)." *Hispania* 74, no. 2 (1991): 298–304.

Johnson, Randal. *Cinema Novo × 5: Masters of Contemporary Brazilian Film.* Austin: University of Texas Press, 1984.

————. *The Film Industry in Brazil: Culture and the State.* Pittsburgh: University of Pittsburgh Press, 1987.

José, Emiliano, and Oldack Miranda. *Lamarca: O capitão da guerrilha.* São Paulo: Global Editora, 1980.

Katz, Jonathan. *The Invention of Heterosexuality.* New York: Dutton, 1995.

King, John. *Magical Reels: A History of Cinema in Latin America.* London: Verso, 1990.

Lins, Ronaldo Lima. *O teatro de Nelson Rodrigues: Uma realidade em agonia.* Rio de Janeiro: Livraria Francisco Alves Editora, 1978.

Lispector, Clarice. *A hora da estrela.* Rio de Janeiro: J. Olympio, 1977.

"List of the Tortures Most Commonly Used in Brazil and Uruguay." In *State of Siege,* directed by Constantin Costa-Gavras, written by Franco Solinas; screenplay translated by Brooke Leveque; documents translated by Raymond Rosenthal, 198–202. New York: Ballantine Books, 1973.

Lockhart, Melissa. "*Beijo no asfalto* and Compulsory Heterosexuality." *Gestos* 17 (1994): 147–158.

————. "Nelson Rodrigues." In *Latin American Writers on Gay and Lesbian Themes: A Bio-Critical Sourcebook,* ed. David William Foster, 370–374.

Machos, Mistresses, Madonnas: Contesting the Power of Latin American Gender Imagery. Ed. Marit Melhuus and Kristi Anne Stølen. London: Verso, 1996.

Mafre, Inês S. "Passeiozinho com Pagu e outras viagens poéticas." *Travessia* [Florianópolis] 21 (1990): 93–104.

Marcos, Plínio. *Barrela.* São Paulo: Editora Símbolo, 1976.

Meyer, Richard. "Rock Hudson's Body." In *Inside/Out: Lesbian Theories, Gay Theories,* ed. Diana Fuss, 258–288. Bloomington: Indiana University Press, 1991.

Michalski, Yan. *O teatro sob pressão: Uma frente de resistência.* Rio de Janeiro: Jorge Zahar Editor, 1985.

Mott, Luiz. "Brazil." In *Encyclopedia of Homosexuality,* ed. George Haggerty. 2nd ed. New York: Garland Publishing, forthcoming.

Moyano, María José. *Argentina's Lost Patrol: Armed Struggle 1969–1979.* New Haven: Yale University Press, 1995.

Patarra, Judith Lieblich. *Iara: Reportagem biográfica.* Rio de Janeiro: Rosa dos Tempos, 1992.

Perlongher, Néstor. *O negócio do michê: Prostituição viril em São Paulo.* São Paulo: Brasiliense, 1987.

Pile, Steven. *The Body and the City: Psychoanalysis, Space and Subjectivity.* London: Routledge, 1996.

Reis, Roberto. "Aluísio Azevedo." In *Latin American Writers on Gay and Lesbian Themes: A Bio-Critical Sourcebook,* ed. David William Foster, 49.

———. "João Guimarães Rosa." In *Latin American Writers on Gay and Lesbian Themes: A Bio-Critical Sourcebook,* ed. David William Foster, 385–386.

Roberts, Shari. "The Lady in the Tutti-Frutti Hat: Carmen Miranda, a Spectacle of Ethnicity." *Cinema Journal* 32, no. 3 (1993): 3–23.

Russo, Vito. *The Celulloid Closet: Homosexuality in the Movies.* Rev. ed. New York: Harper & Row, 1987. Orig. 1981.

Schoenbach, Peter J. "Plínio Marcos: Reporter of Bad Times." In *Dramatists in Revolt: The New Latin American Theater,* ed. Leon F. Lyday and George W. Woodyard, 243–257. Austin: University of Texas Press, 1976.

Sebreli, Juan José. *La era del fútbol.* Buenos Aires: Editorial Sudamericana, 1998. Orig. *Fútbol y masas.* Buenos Aires: Editorial Galerna, n.d.

Sedgwick, Eve Kosofsky. *Epistemology of the Closet.* Berkeley: University of California Press, 1990.

Silverman, Kaja. *The Subject of Semiotics.* New York: Oxford University Press, 1983.

Simis, Anita. *Estado e cinema no Brasil.* São Paulo: Annablume Editora, 1996.

Simpson, Mark. *Male Impersonators: Men Performing Masculinity.* London: Cassell, 1994.

Sipple, Diane. "Terrorist Acts and 'Legitimate' Torture in Brazil: *How Nice to See You Alive.*" *Discourse* 17, no. 1 (Fall 1994): 77–92.

Sklar, Robert. *Film: An International History of the Medium.* New York: Harry N. Abrams, 1993.

Slater, Candace. *Dance of the Dolphin: Transformation and Disenchantment in the Amazonian Imagination.* Chicago: University of Chicago Press, 1994.

Stam, Robert, and Ismail Xavier. "Transformation of National Allegory: Brazilian Cinema from Dictatorship to Redemocratization." In *Resisting Images: Essays on Cinema and History,* ed. Robert Sklar and Charles Musser, 279–307. Philadelphia: Temple University Press, 1990.

Sylvio Back: Filmes noutra margem. Curitiba: Governo do Paraná, Secretaria de Estado da Cultura, 1992.

Szoka, Elzbieta. "The Spirit of Revolution in Contemporary Brazilian Theatre: An Interview with Plínio Marcos." *TDR: The Drama Review* 34, no. 1 (1990): 70–83.

Tasker, Yvonne. *Spectacular Bodies: Gender, Genre and the Action Cinema.* New York: Routledge, 1993.

Theweleit, Klaus. *Male Fantasies.* Trans. Stephen Conway, in collaboration with Erica Carter and Chris Turner. Minneapolis: University of Minnesota Press, 1987.

Valdés, Hernán. *Tejas Verdes: Diario de un campo de concentración en Chile.* Barcelona: Editorial Ariel, 1974.

Vieira, Adriana, and Deborah Giannini. "Super-heroínas." *Revista Folha,* 22-12-96, on-line service.

Viñas, David. *Indios, ejército y frontera.* Mexico City: Siglo XXI Editores, 1982.

West, Dennis. *Contemporary Brazilian Cinema.* Albuquerque: Latin American Institute, University of New Mexico, 1984.

Zavarzadeh, Masud. *Seeing Films Politically.* Albany: State University of New York Press, 1991.

Zeitlin, Marilyn A. "[Interview with Noam Chomsky:] El Salvador and Global Colonialism." In *Arte bajo presión: El Salvador 1980–presente,* 95–112. Tempe: Arizona State University, Museum of Art, 1995.

Index